DYLON P. CHARLES

NEW YOUNG
STRANGER

The Discovery

authorHOUSE

AuthorHouse™
1663 Liberty Drive
Bloomington, IN 47403
www.authorhouse.com
Phone: 833-262-8899

Published by AuthorHouse   05/07/2021

ISBN: 978-1-5246-9197-4 (sc)
ISBN: 978-1-5246-9198-1 (e)

Library of Congress Control Number: 2017907541

Print information available on the last page.

Any people depicted in stock imagery provided by Thinkstock are models, and such images are being used for illustrative purposes only. Certain stock imagery © Thinkstock.

This book is printed on acid-free paper.

To my loving mother, Judith R. Charles

Acknowledgments

I want to thank God for investing the time and patience through the late-night and early morning hours to make this book possible.

I also thank God for the understanding and knowledge through the exposition He has given me to share with others His Word.

Special thanks to everyone who prayed for me, encouraged me, and stood by me through the publication of this book.

May God's richest blessings be bestowed upon everyone who reads this book, and may it help and strengthen your faith as it challenges you to believe the deep truths.

With love,
Dylon Pharez Charles

Contents

Section 1

The Discovery

Section 2

My Place in God

Section 3

Looking at Life

Section 4

Destiny Eternal

Introduction

New Young Stranger: The Discovery is the epiphany of discovering and rediscovering God in us and we in Him. It shows us who we are, who God is and is to us, and who we should be to Him. The discovery is like a hidden mystery of the things we may experience in our lives. This is a personal journey with God from the time we become saved and forward to eternity. The journey will have ups and downs, such as when the revelation of our faults, weaknesses, and strengths are revealed to us.

Some of us may be searching; we may think, Am I gaining on the things I long to gain more of, or am I just going around in circles? We all have dreams and hopes we want fulfilled, but at times we fall because of our own ways and words or simply because we have not committed our thoughts to the Lord, that He may establish it in His honor. This book will help put us back on the road of progression. It conveys a message to bolster our confidence in our callings and in our individual lives.

When I gave my life to Christ, I was set on a journey of discovery. Through His Word, I discovered who He was and also who I'm meant to be. Along that journey, I began to discover the old me that was becoming new in Christ. I discovered my past ways of sin and error as I was on this new journey of holiness and righteousness. The more I studied the Word of God, the more I discovered things that I couldn't understand with a carnal mind; I now took on a spiritually sound mind in Christ. Through those moments on my journey, I discovered my strengths and weaknesses.

Are you a new young stranger starting off in the things of God to become more of what He has called you to be? If so, this is a good time to look at life with the perspective in which Christ looks, observing ways of life and making wise choices to the eternal things of glory that He has laid up for us.

"Hear my prayer, O Lord, and give ear unto my cry; hold not thy peace at my tears: for I am a stranger with thee, and a sojourner, as all my fathers were." (Psalm 39:12)

Section 1

The Discovery

From transformation to the understanding of the discovery, this section opens the initial stage of the new young stranger's journey, as the in-depth understanding of our lives comes from darkness to light in Christ. We can liken ourselves to structures built by our heavenly Master.

"Transformation—All in All"

The first brick laid down is transformation, which pivots the new structure on the solid understanding that the old ways must go through a process of change, from internal to external. This brick must be firm and well grounded, gaining the strength of being unshakeable and unmovable.

"Spiritual Inner Strength"

The second brick, laid upon the first, is spiritual inner strength. From here on, as transformation takes place, removing the old things within, the new things fill the place of the old, occupying that space so it will not return again. It has lost its place, power, and function.

"The Sealing Identity"

The third brick, the sealing identity, is essential as things take shape and form to reflect the meaning, purpose, and person who is altering shape into God's likeness. Now the stamp that authenticates ownership and belonging represents the Overseer of our souls. This seal is placed on the inside to function and to guard the new things that maintain a clean, prestigious, and well-labeled structure.

"Spotless, Sinless"

Brick four—spotless, sinless—brings to our knowledge the things that we should keep out of reach. "Spotless, sinless" alerts us that there are consequences if the structure being built is decaying and defiled with the things of which we once were fond (and may be on open display) of. By faith we will be able to resist and build a hedge of protection around us so that safety and security is always our top priority and on demand.

"The Discovery"

Once the structure is built on these elements, a discovery will take place, where we know how and where we stand. The discovery is much like a journey in time that is steered by the Master so that it is completed, step by step. If we need to make changes and adjustments, the steps will be there again for us to follow.

Transformation—All in All

Transformation opens to us the understanding of the internal working of the Holy Spirit with the process of change, as we are revealed in Christ and He in us. We can discover ourselves—but to what extent and to what eternal purpose and merit? When we discover ourselves in God as "new young strangers," however, we don't know how much of a transformation will take place in us by the proportion of our faith. We will begin to discover who we were all along, waiting to be revealed in God.

Transformation is internal and is the continuous working of the Holy Spirit in our lives at the inception of salvation—the born-again process (John 3:3–7). Who you used to be (in the flesh) doesn't matter when you are transformed by the coursed path of a new life that guarantees eternal life. Transformation now means that we have become and are becoming new creatures in Christ, inheriting heavenly spiritual rights and gifts (Galatians 5:22–23). This allows us to approach God boldly to talk to Him as a Father. It allows us to receive gifts that we shouldn't let anyone or anything to take from us, having passed from the things that led to spiritual death to the things that lead to life everlasting in God. This is the discovery that begins as a new young stranger.

The discovery begins when we come to Christ, who is the way, the truth, and the life. He reveals Himself to us and in us, and we discover ourselves in Him. He works within our minds, hearts, souls, and spirits; He works internally by guiding our lives to the depths of the truth. Christ desires that we be like Him, fully grown up and nurtured into His perfection. The

3

process is on our part as we depend on Him, becoming submissive in every way of our lives that by Him we are able to be of difference to the world.

God calls us to holiness because we are born of a sinful nature, in which the things of the world influence us and keep us in the darkness to which our souls are bound. Even in our minds, a renewal process must take place as the Spirit works in us (Ephesians 4:23). We cannot gain more of God if we do not open and submit ourselves to Him. This is where transformation begins and continues. We must abide in Christ, and there is no other way we can reach our eternal destination in heaven except through Him.

Such discoveries show us clearly the exposure of our sins and how disgusting they were, and it also shows us the pureness and richness of God's love—having sent His Son to pay such a heavy price. All our sins He bore— those of the past and those that we may still be overcoming. Overcoming sin is a progressive work that bears and awakes our consciousness, and it tells us that we can no longer be ignorant of our weaknesses but must instead deal with them the moment they present themselves. Often our failures, words, and deeds are the things that made us weak and kept us in sin's darkness. Chances are that if we don't deal with them, we may find ourselves again falling and being overtaken by them.

As new young strangers in God, we must be on the lookout while at the same time keeping up our faith by studying and praying to God always (Luke 18:1). If we have just started off, we may find ourselves being weak and may think that we are unable to make it. But as we continue, we will discover the strength that God provides for us. Many people today are fearful of being Christians, simply because they believe they will fall off, that they are not strong enough to hold their ground. They see only their weaknesses and not God's strength. This is what the devil wants people to believe. But if we truly come to Christ and are determined to remain, then He will give enough strength to be sustained.

Every soul to Christ is precious and of great worth, since He died for all lives. As we value our lives so much more, He values our lives now sealed in Him. Continuing on, we begin to see who our real enemy was and is—and also how much he hates us and was all along trying to destroy us. But then the love of God prevailed, and now we see clearly how Christ died for us. We can now appreciate Him more than we ever did.

Our weaknesses are no longer hidden from us, but as we keep on studying and reading, we will begin to see that the Word is our source of strength, wisdom, knowledge, and understanding. We now experience the all in all in God as He searches and proves us. He searches out and tries us so that we can gain strength and be kept in the things that we have committed to Him. We have committed our lives to Him, and He will teach us to love Him through all our weaknesses. We must strive to overcome our weaknesses, and He will help us out of our troubles.

The closer we draw to God, the closer He will draw to us and avail Himself to us. We cannot refrain or be broken down by what others may think and say; instead, we must look to the new things that He will do in our lives unto His glory. We must forget the things of the past as if they never happened. If we hold on to our past, it may hold on to our future.

Learning to let go is what Christ will teach us. Many are the things of the past that we have been through, and now we can see clearly who God is—and we can see the person He has called us to be.

Transformation also changes the course of our lives, aligning and preparing us for future things, as our understanding about things we couldn't see, hear, or understand becomes vividly clear to us. From the moment we are transformed in Christ, we must build up ourselves in humbleness and diligence every day. This is the time when we experience God's love, grace, and mercy in ways that we never thought could have been experienced. Now we know and understand what others have been talking about and experiencing all along.

Transformation is a serious aspect of our lives because it draws the line of separation between wills, desires, and feelings and a holy calling

> *Without transformation, it would be impossible for the old person to become the new person in Christ.*

of profoundness. Our lives shouldn't be seen as just a separation from the things of the world. They should be seen as a light of love and hope for the salvation of those who are lost within the things of the world. Our change not only affects us; it affects others. We must also show others the truth as often as we can.

When we thought that we knew God in the world (while living in sin), we now understand that we knew about Him and that this was a way to get to know Him. Now others are our concern because we see how the world presents itself in ways of deceitfulness. This presentation seems to fulfill things for a while, but it ultimately leads others to a bitter end.

The process of life as a new young stranger may be challenging and provocative in every way, but we must not give up or cast aside such precious things. The present life may seem to be so full of affliction and pressure that the things we want to change may take time and be a process. Patience, however, is what we must learn, and we must ensure that we don't do things in haste without the proper foundation. Because God knows and understands the times and seasons of all things, we, in turn, will know when the time is right.

Putting things into the way they should be may seem hopeless at first, but God will prove Himself to be faithful in all ways at all times—even when we don't seem to understand or have patience. He knows the intent of our hearts, and He also knows the intent of the spiritual enemy of our souls. But in all things and in all ways He will make a way so that we are able to bear and escape the snares of the devil. We are not alone in this; He is with us, even though at times it may seem like He doesn't see or hear us. In those times, when He appears to be hidden, He is actually right there at our call, and He will show up in ways that we weren't expecting.

By faith in His words and promises and in His Spirit of assurance, we know that we have gained the things that make us free in Christ. Having faith at this time and forever is most necessary as we learn and develop to trust God at His word. Without faith, we cannot overcome or move ahead and let go of the past. Though we may bear the consequences of our sins, we must never see these consequences as proof that He hasn't forgiven us.

Faith is the key for us to be encouraged of God, and it is also the key that keeps God encouraging us.

We must know also that the target of the devil is to break us down in our minds of the things that we have done and allowed in our lives. Now we see and understand how real our enemy is and how we have almost missed out on all of the good things to which God has called us. We can never fully understand or see the things that we ought to see unless we are in the Spirit. He shows us the intent of our enemy and teaches us how to pray to counterattack the things that are or may be above our thoughts and feelings, which at the end may seem to aim at breaking us down and taking us out.

Christ has paid the measure of all forgiveness of our sins. We cannot be ignorant and think that the devil will forget our past, but we must be strong, not allowing him to have an advantage over us or to use it as his point of affliction, where we again seem to feel sorry for ourselves for those things for which God has so long forgiven us that we are left frustrated and feeling guilty.

Say the following words to yourself: "My past is not my future." This is something to remember: God has already forgiven and forgotten all these things, and as the scripture says, He has removed them as far as the east is from the west (Psalm 103:12).

It is Christ who died and bore all our sins, and He also is the one who will justify us as the righteousness of God as we walk with Him in the Spirit. Walking in the Spirit is having life and all the things of the Spirit, guiding, guarding, influencing, and keeping us unto His will and purposes.

Who the Son makes free is free indeed (John 8:36). Walk in God, and never look back or give up or give in. Keep the faith of such rich confidence speaking to Him as He so desires to speak with you.

Searched, Deep Within

He that made the mind knows the thoughts; He that made the heart knows its intentions, He that made the soul knows its inner callings, and He that made the spirit knows its strengths and weaknesses. Who we are and who we intend to be is no secret to God. As is the sand upon the shores of the sea, so He knows the number of us by name. He made a proposal to us, and it is this: accept Christ and live, or reject Him and die (spiritually/eternally).

He searches us out by our intentions and wills to see whether we allow wisdom to be a part of us by adherence or allow foolishness by disobedience. Even at transformation, He looks at the sincerity of our hearts and if we are true to ourselves; then the truth of God will begin to take its place in us. As He searches us in His truth, so must we also search ourselves.

God also searches things in life of which our lives will be. He searches out things by His wisdom and knowledge so we are cautioned from falling into snares. He chooses our inheritance for us, even after our own desires (Psalm 47:4). Upon all of that, His favor is bestowed to us. We know now that His searching us out is not to embarrass us but to embrace us when we start in Him unto the end.

Spiritual Inner Strength

Spiritual inner strength opens the understanding that strength from within must exist and that growth in our spiritual walks must touch our minds, hearts, souls, and spirits. Spiritual inner strength bolsters our faith in God that we are not easily and suddenly shaken upon believing His truth, revealed in His Word, against anything that comes up as a challenge.

The perpetuity of our endurance in this spiritual battle depends on well rounded strength that is first spiritual. Christ calls us to be strong, and this calling is a holy calling that measures itself in any situation or battle we face. We are now of the Spirit of God, having sowed the seeds that will bring forth our strength in faith. We need faith in order to overcome them. It's expedient in all ways to have hope toward God by the renewal of His Spirit with the Word. Even if our lives are different and are called to a different vocation, the Spirit of God searches out all things according to God's perfect will, that whatever we are engaged in will work out to be His perfect will for our lives (1 Corinthians 2:10). He searches out wisdom, knowledge, and understanding for our lives. With the guide and strength of the Holy Spirit, we are certain of the things in which we are engaged. This assurance gives us the confidence to continue.

Spiritual inner strength in God gives us daily added wisdom, knowledge, and understanding that keeps and prepares us for what is ahead. To anyone who is weak, God-imparted wisdom can help that person find

Balancing our inner strength keeps us focused, from a spiritual perspective to a natural perspective (buoyancy).

the strength to bring alive all things for a life in Him. He wants us to be wise and not just know that wisdom exists—wise in the things we do and even how we do them. Daily we are faced with challenges, and we must have faith and strength in Him to overcome and stay ahead of the changing things in our lives.

Staying focused in God is key, no matter what situation or circumstance may present itself. Upon all of that, there is the call of faithfulness that adds God's grace to our lives. Faithfulness in keeping ourselves aligned with His Word allows Him to look out for us at all times. He is a present help in the time of trouble (Psalm 46:1; Isaiah 40:29). How can we stand (or expect to stand) if there is no faith and faithfulness? As new young strangers, our minds must be alert and cognizant above the things that will set us back against our wills and desires.

The upkeep of the Word of God in our lives will give us the power we need. As thirsty souls, we always will seek quality time in the Word, knowing what we will reap from sowing it upon our hearts. The knowledge of the Word is good, but it's better when it is applied and met with power. Then it can have an effect in our lives. Rather than being broken down by our weaknesses, the Word will caution us while helping us to move on as the Spirit empowers us within (Ephesians 3:16–20).

Spiritual advantage in our lives is strength that has been tested and proven, that we are determined now to move on as the foundation of our faith has taken its place of assurance. Without the Word of God in our lives, we would not be able to determine the strength and might of the work of the Spirit. We are tested in all points of our lives, even as Christ was. Therefore, an ongoing knowledge and understanding of the Word of God concerning different issues of which the Bible speaks can help us greatly. The Lord our God is our strength and shield (Psalm 28:7). In fact, of this He will defend us as we do our part. We can't say that we are who we are in God, and He is in us, if there is no working of the Spirit's operation in our lives to bring out the good and best fruit that will label us as perfection in Him.

Light has a purpose—to shine—and that means to let all the goodness of God be our determining factor of who we truly are from the inside out.

Though we are tried emotionally, spiritually, physically, and mentally, we can gain strength from the Word because the Word touches all the inner points of our lives that can only truly be refreshed to glory in God. Often when we feel weak as Christians, it's because we are weak from within—the inner person. Our spirits that are now connected to God will, from time to time, become hungry and thirsty for the Word that now gives and sustains its life. The Word of God is Spirit and life (John 6:63).

What determines our strengths and weaknesses? Is it our own words? Is it our deeds? Is it our feelings? Could it be our emotions? If we do not deal with the reactions of these things, it can—and will—have an effect on our lives. Whether the effect is beneficial or adverse tells how weak or strong our faith and will are—either we are mastered by them, or we are the masters of them.

Inner strength, from a spiritual perspective, can help us to deal with things of which we may be afraid or can't seem to fight against. There always are battles to fight in our lives. For those from which we can't always turn away, we deal with in the Spirit. The strength that we have received of the Spirit will bring us victory at the end of our trials. God making a way. (Psalm 18:32)

Christ understands our feelings and the trials we go through. He can relate to them in every possible way. The perfection of our strength is in Him. When we call, He will answer (Jeremiah 33:3). When we thought that no one understood, we were wrong. When we thought that no one would hear us, we were wrong, and when we thought that no one could relate, we were wrong. God is the strength of our lives as we abide in Him (Psalm 27:1). He is the strength of our hearts (Psalm 73:26), and He is the strength of our souls (Psalm 118:14; 138:3). Always remember that the joy of the Lord is your strength (Nehemiah 8:10).

Inner Calling

We all have inner callings (a desire that seeks fixation or satisfaction from something), those that we understand and those we may not understand. As physical spiritual human beings in God, we have both. Our physical beings can be influenced by the spiritual call that God makes in our lives by His Spirit. As the Spirit of truth at acceptance works in our lives, He gives us a heavenly desire to seek Him within our souls and spirits, the depth and height of which will be fulfilled when we put on immortality.

It is not just what we see, hear, or feel but what we hope for, the things not yet within our grasps. There is one true inner calling that can be fully satisfied solely from the Life Giver, Christ Jesus. The best day of our lives will be when the fulfillment of our inner calling in God comes to past eternally.

While we are pilgrims here on earth, the things by which our lives are touched should never allow us to lose focus on the heavenly. Even as we are amazed by things here on earth, we should recognize that the heavenly will be immeasurably greater as our beings are caught up in the revealed hidden mystery. This will be the full extent of inner calling and the presence of things to come.

The Sealing Identity

The sealing identity speaks of how God has us sealed in Him and that His seal represents us as bright lights shining for Him. His seal on us is a seal of preservation unto eternity.

Everyone who comes to Christ will be given a new identity.

It starts deep within the heart, and the actions and outcomes are manifested in righteousness. The inner transition of our new identities tells us who we were, who we are, and who we are led to be.

The Spirit of God is our seal to identify us as children of God (Ephesians 1:13; 4:30). No one can claim to be a child of God unless they first come to Christ and has assurance by the Spirit of God that so abides within him or her. (Romans 8:9) When this is so, we will know because the Spirit of God will begin to work within us. He teaches us to fight the devil and overcome the world and the will of the flesh. He also teaches us to love each other and care for each other. To obtain and maintain our identity in Christ, we must allow the Spirit to function in our lives daily. When we set things in order in our lives (the things that so influence the Spirit's work and presence in our lives), He can always manifest Himself to us and through us.

> *The inner reflection of our hearts reveals the ways of the hidden contents within, which mirrors the likelihood of Christ in us shining through.*

Our identities are shielded by our faith in God, that He looks out for us because His mark is upon us (Ephesians 6:16). Our identities are not hidden if we are truly in Christ, as we are apt to make wise decisions and choices. Our identities speak on behalf of us, our characters, and our attitudes. Keeping up our identities in God is not without testing and trials; at times they may seem to want to break us down and take us out—God forbid.

Our identities are not concealed—and shouldn't be, if we are lights in Christ. Our enemy knows that, and he will try to bring us down, even starting the battle within us and around us. With all things, God will make a way of escape, that by His Spirit we can be renewed and have access. No more are we the fleshy pleasers of ourselves; now we must strive within to please God with our words and deeds, that in all things we are kept holy and matured unto the things we are called unto.

Our identities are a light in God that should never be put out or become dull, even though we are tested daily with different circumstances. Our lights are brighter when the Spirit begins to work for us as much as we abide and submit ourselves to Him. Light in God has no darkness and because Christ is light, the more we liken ourselves to Him, the more our lives become brighter lights, with wisdom in a darkened and deceptive world. Consider this: there are different types of light—those that are bright, those that glow, and those that are dim.

We always must be on the lookout—for our lives as well as for others—and always go before God in intercessory prayer that our prayers can be words of deliverance and encouragement to those of broken and weak hearts. It will take endurance to maintain such a light of faith, grace, and mercy; we must be careful and watchful, lest the devil, our adversary, beguile us with the things of which we have little or no knowledge of.

Our identities are most precious to Christ, as they should be to us—what and how we do things will reflect on His name, such that many who look to us may become doubters and disbelievers. Our identities serve as a way to encourage unbelievers to become believers, teaching them the concept and precept of the things of God, in the spirit of meekness (Galatians 6:1).

Our lives are as open books, waiting to be searched, and our approval is not needed. Whether or not we think others aren't looking, they really are. Can our lights be hidden if they are to be lights upon a hilltop? No, they are not hidden, and that will raise questions, with others seeking answers. God has called us to preserve ourselves in Christ, so that there will be no reproach if we fall.

If we walk daily by faith and do and say the things that will keep us firm, we won't create a breach between us and God, such that we can't find our identities or know where we stand in Him. It is incumbent upon us as Christians to know where we stand in God and where He stands in us. We cannot live as blind guides, not knowing where we came from or where we're heading. We sometimes may fall short and feel as if our identities are shaken, but we shouldn't give up or give in to the thoughts that provoke us to turn away from God. If we care about our souls, we should confess our faults, repent, and move on.

Strength is needed when we search our lives, examining ourselves before God. Our examination is for our own good, that we may know what caused us to fall and what will keep us from falling again. The things we ignore or pay little attention to can open a door, leaving a mark upon us, such that our light in Christ begins to go out, and being out of zeal, we can't muster the strength to humble ourselves before God again.

We never stand alone because Christ promised never to leave or forsake us. He has sent His angels to keep us in the right way so we are not led and taken by the devil's tactics, which we can't see openly. The angels of the Lord look out for us by protecting us from evil spirits that try to destroy our lives. We must be aware of such things and know that we are maintained spiritually in Christ's name.

We cannot be ignorant of the things that can leave open a door for the devil to manipulate us, even those things that we can't see or understand (unless the Spirit reveals them to us).

This is where we stand, and faith is the aspect of our calling. We can better understand how important it is for us to depend on God and maintain our faith in Him. When we do, we are confident and can speak boldly to Him. Pure confidence shows that we are of the truth and that the condemnation of the things of the world is no longer a part of us—neither are we taken into captivity by it. The confidence we have gained in God by our faith should be kept strong and focused on the things that will carry us on to the end (1 John 3:21; 5:14).

We sometimes have to face the things we hate as God prepares us for greater and deeper things in Him. He will use the tests and trials that we bear with faithfulness to carry us to those greater and deeper things in the Spirit that will bring us to perfection. By understanding the works of the flesh and the fruit of the Spirit, we truly can do so. How did those who went on before us come to perfection? By their words we are now encouraged to keep the faith and be made strong. We are tested to keep the light shining. If we have no testing, what will become of us? If we are to live godly in Christ, there will be a test in which we will have a testimony to save and encourage others.

Our lives as lights can cause someone who has a will and desire for the things of God to continue, perhaps just when that person might have thought of giving up. The battles are not ours alone; they are others' battles as well, and we can send forth a much greater light to a darkened and sinful world. As we look from the place where God started us to the place where we now stand, can we truly say that we have shined our lights and that our identities are still sealed in Him?

It is not our past or great works we have done that will get us into heaven even if we turn away from God; it is our current status in Him, which we have maintained through the years. God is pleased with our work and has approved of it, but what He loves most is when those who have started with Him continue with Him, as His grace still abounds. He searches out all things by His Spirit to make all things fair when He judges. He searches out our lives with grace and mercy, that we can adhere to His calling and Word, working out our salvation with fear and trembling that keeps our souls' way in check (Philippians 2:12).

The Spirit of God is He who will promote and present us to Christ on the day when He returns to take us home. He will come and stay as long as time exists while Christ tarries, so that we are not lost and unable to find the way to approach the throne of God boldly. We should all know where we stand and should keep on standing, while remaining solely dependent on Him so we can comfort others.

The Spirit knows when we are tired and how much we can bear, and so He refreshes us daily (2 Corinthians 4:16). As we keep our identities sealed in God, so are we preserved and persuaded that nothing that exists—whether in the heavens or the earth or of things to come that we can't see or control—shall stand in our way to separate us from our God, through the pains and suffering that Christ bore upon His body so we can have that same eternal peace. Sealed are we who are in the Spirit of God. The fruit we bear can speak for itself.

Dylon P. Charles

As We Grow in Christ

From where we were to where we are now (and still are hoping to be), we can look back to see what God has taught us through the process of our upbringing. When we were as babes in Christ, our thoughts still betrayed us to contrary actions, but now that growth is taking place, we are sure that we are maturing.

As we grow in Christ, we will see that the things that we once loved and thought we would never get over are no longer a driving force; we have no desire to obey its will. As we grow in Christ we will remember that, at times, we cried when we discovered who we were in the flesh and where we now dwell in the Spirit. We now know that we were wrong all along, now that we've discovered what's right.

As we grow in Christ, the inner changes will be externally known and become even more evident to those among us. Light is never hidden, and in our hearts, it will shine even when others don't understand the work Christ is performing within us.

As we grow in Christ, our relationship to Him becomes a treasure that we don't want to lose. As we grow in Christ, our trust in Him bolsters our faith so all things are possible, even through the grimmest of situations.

As we grow in Christ, we become one with Him—we in Him, and He in us. As we grow in Christ, we understand what He felt and went through. It is good that in our youth, we seek God, and we bear and overcome the things that will make us perfect men and women of God later in life.

Spotless, Sinless

"Spotless, sinless" encourages us to desire a fondness toward righteousness and become haters of sin (not people). Many of us who know God may have desired to go deeper and higher in Him, but it all starts with us alleviating sin, which commonly causes us to fall. Any sin that we can't seem to overcome complicates our relationship with our heavenly Father, when we are consciously aware but ignore dealing with it. Carefulness in everything would stand out, as the knowledge of God's Word is hidden deeper in our hearts.

"For all have sinned, and come short of the glory of God." (Romans 3:23)

Human weakness, with a feeling of compromise, can make it harder at times for some to stop sinning because they are held by the cords of it. Do we strive not to sin, or do we say we can't stop, and by our confessions we strengthen our weaknesses? Do we say at times, "Is it me or humanity?" and we find ourselves battling with our thoughts? There always are battles, as little as they may seem, and if we don't deal with them early, they may get bigger. Understanding human weakness shows us that we need to be dependent on One who is greater than we are—God Himself. As new babes in Christ, we need that initial strength of being prepared for the things ahead, even if we can't see or touch them before they come our way, but we know they are inevitable.

It is God's call on our lives to be holy, to be spotless, sinless of the things that can add to or lead to deeper sins in our life. This is where the process begins—if we are willing to allow Him to help us get over them.

> *The pursuit of peace, holiness, and righteousness in Christ is the understanding of the heart that knows its place of calling in God.*

To overcome a pattern of sin in our lives, we must first identify the sin and understand what the sin does to us and how it makes us think and feel. If we don't recognize sin as sin, chances are we may never deal with it.

In a spiritually darkening world, there is a safe haven in God. First, though, we must understand that we are weak and are in need of His help. Battling sin encompasses all that is ungodly and unrighteous. Can we attain a level of righteousness, where a certain pattern of sin no longer overtakes or overcomes us anymore? Yes, it is possible and attainable.

As we are human beings with a human nature, we must, as new young strangers, acquire and maintain consistent control of the things that have a sinful calling and are determined to destroy our lives. We comprehend the stage of the battle within us by the things we see, hear, and feel, and it's evident which of those that seem appealing and pleasant are snares for our souls. We must depend on the Holy Spirit at all times because He will be working within us to bring out the good fruit of nature in Christ. His mission is to comfort but also to strengthen us when we face our worst and trying situations, which, with our mortal temperament, we may not be able to hold back. He awakes our consciousness to shun the things that are a means of destroying the pathway that leads to life. Which pathway are we on? This is a question we should ask ourselves from time to time.

Though we live in a world that has more of a sinful nature (and is ever increasing), ceasing to fight against sin to be spotless is not an option we can quickly give up. Through the process of becoming strong, we are tested in all ways, even by our own words—speaking of the good we will do and of the things of a sinful nature we say we wouldn't do. Testing brings out patience and awakens our dependence on calling God to make a way of escape, to preserve our souls from being taken by the enemy. With such testing, our weaknesses and strengths are highlighted, that we may guard ourselves from falling. There is an outer guarding and an inner guarding that are dependent on each other. The Word of God on which we meditate strengthens us from within, so that the influences around us may be in subjection. There is a will also—a will either to shun or rebuke or a will to give in. There, the wrestling for our souls is heightened as we stand firm upon the Word, having the confidence of a strong mind.

Our minds can be influenced by the things we see, which at times may influence everything we feel. Keeping our minds guarded by the Spirit who awakes our consciousness can measure our weaknesses or strengths by the way we view and perceive things. A weak mind can be easily used and manipulated by unconscious and impulsive things, as shown in our actions.

As much as we are of a human nature, we are also spiritual beings, and the things we allow to influence our lives are the things the Spirit of God can act upon to keep us saved in Him. As spiritual beings, we must understand the spiritual calling of both soul and spirit, so our minds and hearts can have a desire for heavenly things that keeps us operating by the Spirit concerning all things that stand as guards over our lives. Spiritual things in God safeguard our lives when we allow them to take a place in us.

Knowing our place in God and His place in us is of utmost importance to help us see things the way He sees them for our lives. We shouldn't live our lives blindfolded, ignoring what He stands for, and come up with our own intentions and ways to supersede the things He has laid down. Let us follow Christ that we may be "spotless, sinless" when He appears to take us home to glory (Ephesians 5:27; 2 Peter 3:12–14).

Conscience-Taken

Conscience-taken, heartbroken, remorse spoken, and soul-shaken—we are these at times. Guilt concealed now revealed, repentance made sins forgiven. From sinners to saints, some have made it before us and stayed in it, but others betrayed it. The consciences of many in the world today are snared in the untruth, in the deceitfulness and lust of the world. How do we know what the truth is, and how can we be sure of it? By believing in the one and only Son of God—and this is not overstated.

Guilt may be a hard thing to deal with, especially if the measure of it grows to a point that we never thought it would reach. At one point, we are all conscience-taken, as the things in our lives reveal themselves to us. To be conscience-taken of our ways is not at all a bad thing, if we intend to change it. The guilt feelings may seem bad, but there is forgiveness with God.

Carrying the weight of guilt, when we are conscience-taken about it, can bring us back to a place we once were or from which we were delivered. Feeling guilty about something is like having guilt written all over us, and others sometimes easily see it. Better to feel guilty of our sins and deal with them than to carry the weight of it within us. Now that our consciences are lightened, let the truth shine through us, and by it we will forever stand.

The Discovery

5

If our lives are hidden from us, the discovery awaits. Day by day, in the time we spend with ourselves before God, we can see deeper things in our lives, things we never thought existed. God wants us to search ourselves for the cause of our faith to know how we stand and how we should stand.

The discovery of our lives hangs upon the knowledge of who we are internally, not only what we see in the mirror. At times, what we see ourselves to be could bring about different feelings and emotions. The big question is, do we know who we are? When we search deep within, who do we find? Do we find the person we once were, the person we are, or the person we are working toward and hoping to be? Have we searched deep within ourselves or are we to busy? Have we identified the strengths of good that will build us up, or have we found the bad that has been breaking us down, that we can't seem to conquer and put under submission?

Our human lives are open to us when we take time to understand ourselves internally. The discovery of God in us (and we in Him) helps us build the confident men and women of God who are called and used to fill the positions that our imaginations can't always fathom.

Every once in a while, as we grow, we will discover the profound meaning of being discovered by God within ourselves.

Some may say, "How can I be who I am called to be when a part of me says I would make it to the end, and another part of me says I will fail and might not be able to stand? A part of me says I can't go on, and I feel like quitting, and another part of me says I can do all things through Christ, which strengthens me. A part of me says all things are possible, as long as I keep on believing, and another part of me doubts the same things I want to change and hope for."

Within our hearts are the things waiting to be discovered as the issues of life concerning our needs and wants are set straight before us (Proverbs 4:23).

What, then, defines the human call? The human call tells us that as long as we live, there are needs and wants we must answer, and if they aren't answered, the way things should work in our lives will be impeded. Though not every need and want should be answered, we weigh the things that are necessary and expedient. Answering the human call is not always easy because of the things we can't see as yet that are as important as our needs—the things that are unforeseen that we must make time to deal with.

We cannot always keep tabs on our needs and wants, and sometimes it may seem as if we can't keep fulfilling them, even on the straight pathway of life. This is the moment when Christ gives us a helping hand. As much as we have life, we should discover the good things within us because as we grow older, we will see and feel things as changes begin to take place. But can we really know, while we are young, who we are going to be? Many of us may have started off in different directions than we thought we would have been, and as time passed, we discovered that the gifts we possess is of something else. It's where we want to be, what we want to do, and where God will take us. The human call is great as we aspire to every dream possible before us.

We all are searching in this life. While some search the fulfillment of their destiny in this world, others search deeper for the truth of God. Even while others search for answers, they find something else that has an ongoing comfort for a while. Our souls always long for something or someone in which to find comfort. Our souls are touched and most sensitive to the things that are deep. In lifting up and opening our souls to God, we will see how thirsty they were and how thirsty they will be from the first taste. God understands the soul and spirit of humans and that they want to discover things. When we allow them to find Him, He will reveal Himself to us. The discovery is deep and grows deeper when we find Christ. He works from within us because within us, the issues of life are mostly felt.

Deep is the understanding when we discover who we are and even deeper when we discover ourselves in Him. The many who have not discovered themselves as yet should do so—the discovery is waiting on them. Who can tell what God has placed in the heart of a new young stranger?

The Outcome

In every discovery, there is the achievement of the outcome. Either we arise from where we are, if we are in the heart of sin, or we remain in it, according to how we respond to it. We may arise from being locked up within ourselves, thinking there is nothing deeper to be discovered in God. He is the revealer. He shows the light path because He Himself is light.

The outcome to every action should bring about some change, irrespective of the situation. Some things take time, and because of the length of time, we may feel like not doing anything. However, we ought to be outcome-changers of what seems not to be. There is comfort, happiness, and a peace of mind in outcome. No one likes to take an exam and not learn the outcome be with passes. When the person who never had anything does something to change the situation—that person's outcome is of cheer and happiness, as are countless examples in our lives.

So then, what do we want the outcome of our lives to be? Do we want it to be the same as it is or was—things that have lingered, hoping they will change? Do we want it to be one where we can see things clearer than before, now that we have some safety and security? Do we want it to be the outcome where God lives and dwells in us, guiding us always?

An expected end is what He offers—that's what He said in His Word, that through challenges and tests, we must endure all things. The outcome of our lives is in the palm of God's hands. As long as we put our faith in Him, we can watch it grow. And it is not even about our unfortunate past, if we are alive and willing to change things.

Section 2

My Place in God

This is the moment that depicts God's ways, wills, and desires and highlights ours as well, to bring one common output. This puts us on God's map of progression.

"His Will, Our Will"

"His Will, Our Will" is simply God showing us His goodwill unto His purpose that we within would begin to align ourselves from our former wills of sin and ways using our focus now to embrace His which intern will help fulfill ours. At this point, we will understand the eternal will, rather than only this earthly or temporal will. The earthly or temporal will has a new purpose, and that is to bring the outcome of the eternal by what we do to fulfill and build God's kingdom. Now, as a new young stranger, our will is geared toward an eternal purpose.

"Motivated Purposes"

Coming to light of our understanding, we now realize that we are accountable and responsible for fulfilling a heavenly purpose. If we get weak, we must encourage ourselves, by faith in the Lord, that our labor of servitude is not in vain and neither is our confidence wasted. Our interest and determination will be at the forefront of our thinking and our will, as this gives His will, which is now our will, the push forward to rise to fruition. Side by side, they stand, as each compels the other toward the eternal reward at the end.

The will motivates the purpose, as the purpose motivates the will.

"Up Out of Broken Promises and Purposes"

Though our upbringings may be different, and we may have had broken promises and purposes, we must understand that God restores and brings new things to being. So when we start something, quitting because we are hurt—rather than allowing our Master healer to heal our wounds—is without excuse. Failure to try again may determine if our efforts are of true willingness. Confidence is key at this moment, as we unlock our strength and lock down our weaknesses with a new hope that has words of power tied in with it.

"Vision of the Visionary"

Whatever God envisions in heaven, He puts upon our hearts, orchestrating the turns it makes and expanding on it as time passes. Diligence is key here, as the vision of the visionary works hard at what he or she seeks to accomplish. Though some things take time, each process is a process of refining to bring out the best in planning. This is the moment of observation when the visionary puts his or her thoughts to power by committing them to God, that He can ensure a steady and sustainable outcome by consistency to the vision of calling. Such commitment put pieces together to bring out the masterpiece of anything.

"My Place in God"

Nothing and no one should change, shift, or disrupt our place in God, when our state and course of progression is steady. Because accountability and responsibility is ours, we, by faith, should be eager to keep our place in God, if it is challenged by word or deed to the contrary. When time and effort is put into something to arrive at a new place and position on a journey having borne many trials and temptations along the way to get there we should fight never to give up on it easily to anything of the contrary.

Now we will see the eternal weight of our place in God. If we have considered letting up, we should reconsider it. God does not take pleasure in setting aside a structure in which He puts time and effort. Time and chance will come to test us, but even if we falter, we should never utterly turn our backs on our place in God; we should seek ways to restore it.

His Will, Our Will

As heaven orchestrates what should be fulfilled on earth, and as we live, God opens doors to fulfill His will in our lives, as His also is being fulfilled. As it is in heaven, where things are in order, so does God Himself want things to be in order, both for His Kingdom and our own individual lives, even daily. His will and our will should work together when we understand and integrate ours and His.

Understanding God's will in our lives will help us understand our will in His. God's will is not hidden but is revealed to us by His Word. He has an agenda, and in our own lives, we must allow our will to align with His. Each of our lives are designed and destined to fill positions and fulfill purposes, without confusing God's will with ours but allowing His to be first, to lead ours ahead in life. The things we think of doing and then do them, according to the will of God, must be done with efficiency and effectiveness that brings glory to His name.

Learning to put will over opportunity, rather than putting off things that can be done in an instant or at present will gain us more time, if changes in the things that we do are to be made. Our will to God's will, in all things, can allow us to achieve greater outcomes and a peace of mind afterward. Things that are done in the order that He approves will set us forward, rather than regressing or starting over on things that already should have been finished. The progress of things in God is to build a strong foundation that is not shaken. If changes ought to

> *The soul that balances the known will of our heavenly Father will find it easier to balance its own will as well.*

be made, there is always a steady foundation that is hinged by the Spirit of God guiding us. He knows and understands the space and time of when things should be done, and He goes on guiding us on how it should be done.

Leaning on God's understanding opens new ways and means of doing things as we ask for wisdom, knowledge, and understanding in truthfulness. We are never limited in our will by first calling upon Him to help us and continue as we go on. God sees far ahead of us to how things will turn and go. This provides us ways that we can surely accomplish all our goals in Him (Proverbs 3:5–6). All things are held together by Him, and for our lives, He will look out for us in all ways as we continue to trust in Him. Hardly anything will not stand without faith if our faith is not in the Author and Finisher of our faith, which not only satisfies this present life but is fulfilled in eternity. The things that we do must resound in eternity for a sure reward.

Studying the Bible can guide us in dealing and approaching things in God. He is our chief overseer and watcher.

"Except the Lord build the house they labour in vain that built it: except the Lord keep the city the watchman waketh but in vain" (Psalm 127:1). Understanding that He wants to impart His way and will in our lives by principles can help us be more a person of our word to maintain things in order. His wisdom is higher than ours in all ways, and because we are learning to call and depend on Him, we can achieve something greater in the most of limited resources.

With increased and insightful wisdom, the knowledge and understanding of doing things—not for ourselves only but pertaining to the things of God—keeps us ahead in whatever we put our hands to. Rather than being overly challenged by the things we are engaged in, we can manipulate them by having full control that the word of good stewards of God can be spoken of us. Starting a thing but later quitting that thing we so longed to achieve can break our determination. This is the reason why the Spirit revives us in our fainting. Anything that works along with our will, in all good ways, should be allowed, but with patience rather than in haste, weighing out the future advantages and disadvantages.

When we search the ways of doing things, added with the knowledge we have attained as new young strangers in God, it is a good start that comprehensively will allow us a greater outcome in life. Whatever He has called us to do should be done to the best of our ability, not ignoring the fact that unfortunate things may be our test to bring about better and new ways.

From now into the future, as Christ tarries, our objective is to run all the way, having faith that is guarded and daily trusting in God. He never leaves or forsakes us, as we are concerned about His will, and He, in return, will make our will evident from the initiation of simple thoughts to the working of our hands. He minds our business. Christ wants all things to work, as we have sought first the kingdom of God. Knowing this, we are willed, not just by saying things and not just by doing them but by doing them as often as we say them. We must believe in God, having a pure confidence in the things that may seem hard to achieve, lifting our eyes to the hill from where comes all our strength in Christ Jesus our Lord. With all things in order, His will be our will also.

Equity Balance

Leaning on God's understanding brings balance while we also learn His ways. There are all kinds of needs in life that must be met—spiritual, physical, social, emotional, and financial—and we must be able to balance them. However, the spiritual aspect which is in Christ is the utmost priority governing all other things as we continue to live by faith.

Sometimes life's situations try to maneuver our will to think that things aren't balanced as they should be. We should never let the situation manipulate us. We must gain control of the situation. Then there is the time factor in which we sometimes wish we had more of—we must allow ourselves to be refreshed by daily.

Equity balance does not occur on its own; it takes will to ensure that all things are done as efficiently as they can be. Balancing our lives is a process, and learning to deal with situations at an accountable age can help us to apply this in other fields also. We must stay focused on situations in our lives and make necessary changes, without the hassle of added frustration. Equity balance has various stages as we grow, but if it is in God, we can be sure we will see far off into the future as visionaries.

Motivated Purposes

It's easier to motivate ourselves when we know the purpose and calling. Motivated purposes aligns things the way they should be in God, so we then are sure about the very specific purpose to which we are called. With clear understanding of the purpose, we understand what He has given us in plan and design, and when discouragement kicks in, we are capable of motivating ourselves over it by faith. For anything to be achievable, sacrifices must be made. The keys to motivated purposes are as follows :

1. Find your purpose in God and life. Identify what you are called to do and be in life.

2. Understand your purpose. Gain insight that with a solid foundation of the known purpose, your will over setbacks are superseded by faith and confidence.

3. Act on your purpose. Now that your goals are set and purpose understood, allow yourself to accomplish each one by speaking to yourself as Christ is now your life coach. In other words, lean on God's encouraging words and speaking them forth daily.

Find your purpose in God and then motivate yourself in all ways and at all times, allowing the Spirit to be your guide. Every purpose is established by counsel, and our Counselor is God. The discovery of the hidden mystery for your life will unfold as He searches all things predestined for your life.

Pray that God will reveal His purpose for your life, knowing and understanding that He has called you to something. Our objective as Christians is to live a holy life, but the mission is to win souls. How do we determine what our purpose is, and how do we motivate ourselves? The basics must be clear—we must know to what we are called, and then we can take the next step after that. As new young strangers in God, we must first strengthen ourselves, lest we fall, and engage in all prayers for the mission that is ahead. Even though the mission may seem clear to us, it is a process. We must approach it, having settled on a solid foundation of strength within ourselves.

> *Purpose discovered would give way to fulfilling its aligned course in an open heart and mind, ready to respond.*

Do not be so hindered by your past that you are not motivated to the purpose for which you were called. Remember that all things have become new in Christ Jesus our Lord. Sometimes the thing that breaks down our motivation is of the past we hold on to that we can't seem to find our way ahead and above it. God has already searched deep within us, and He knows the timing of when the engagement of the things that concern Him should begin. Tell your past good-bye by putting up a resistance with the Word, and embrace your future in the things of God. Remember Christ who died and justifies you. Also know that the devil is our accuser and tempter. It is good to understand these things early because many may have seen the clear vision and mission but because of the falter of faith, they never started. Carefulness in all things is good approach that helps us to observe things more clearly.

With a clear vision and mission, we listen to the voice of God to go forward, even as the apostles and disciples did. With the working of the Holy Spirit within us, the things that we thought we couldn't do now become possible. When we learn how to listen and walk with Him, our faith can be maintained. The Holy Spirit is He who enables us to perform the will of God to perfection. He searches us in all things, even the deep things of God, and places it before us in all seasons and times. The things needed and the ways of doing effective work for the Lord and for our lives are before us, and we can take that work to the full extent when we use technology and the media. Our purpose must be pursued daily, as God gives us the grace and strength to do His great will.

Faithfulness in what we are about means building strong confidence in God and also in ourselves. As new young strangers, we must develop and be strong in faith so that what we have attained can be passed on to others, who will come in as new young strangers before God.

Confidently allowing ourselves to do the will of God from the sincerity of our hearts will allow Him to put more things in our care. Our faithfulness is not hidden, and others will see it in the way we do things and the way we may allow things to be. All our work is mounted to God for a remembrance, that He may reward us accordingly.

While running this race of life, we must be encouragers of ourselves, saying the things we will do and seeing them done by faith in the Spirit. Motivated purposes speak also of endurance. If we feel like giving up, or if we can't muster the strength to continue in the thing we have committed to God, that's when we are tested, even by our own words, knowing if we will run all the way through.

God is a patience-tester, and we may have to cry through remaining in His love. "All things work together for good to them that love God, to them who are the called according to His purpose" (Romans 8:28). He that has given us the purpose to fulfill His will, will stand by our side to ensure that we complete it. He is the Author and Finisher of our faith.

Some people don't know why they are living or what their right purpose is. God created us all for a purpose, but until we open ourselves to Him, the purpose can't be revealed. Ephesians 1:11 says, "In whom we have obtained an inheritance, being predestinated according to the purpose of Him who worketh all things after the counsel of His own will."

Build Yourself Up

We weren't always strong, although we might have become so, and because we understand our weaknesses and the demands of it, we compelled ourselves to be even stronger. Build yourself up to the things that will sustain you ahead in life. Put your hand to do it, and in doing so, be diligent and a competent worker.

Regardless of what you hope to build yourself upon or in which category, I want to encourage you. We have foresight so we can see ahead to opportunities that will present themselves and so we make the most of them. Those who build a foundation then can move things around because the strength of it enables them to stand.

You are building yourself to become the person you may have dreamed of becoming since you were a child. You are building yourself to fill positions in life that you were called to fulfill. You are building yourself to have the things God called you to inherit since the foundation of the world. You are building yourself because you have the ability to make it happen. Build yourself up, and trust God's Word, and you will never walk alone.

Up Out Of Broken Promises and Purposes

To whose words of promise have you listened and believed lately? Are they words from the past or the present, or are they words of God? Many of us have been broken, whether by words or deeds, but the time is now to rise up out of broken promises and purposes to embrace those which God now offers.

Every promise has a purpose, and behind every purpose there is an intention. A promise is like a painted picture that compels us to think different things—the reality of what was, what is, and even what we hope for out of such a promise. Some of us have grown from broken promises and purposes, not allowing the present situation to determine what is ahead, but many of us are left in midst of it, longing for a way out and to be healed. Many in the world today are in continuous dismay because of something from their past, and their hearts and minds can't overcome the present pain to see a brighter life.

There is a voice within us that cries out when we are under pressure that wants to break forth because of broken promises and purposes we were promised, but it now seems to have been a false hope. We can't go back in time to fix or change certain things, so we must look forward to fix them in the present.

Promises are expectations that we look forward to, and at times our hope in them can be built up. When you have confidence in a person who makes a promise, you will always look toward the time the promise is fulfilled, but if the promise maker holds back on the promise, your trust can dissolve and you may lose hope. Why is it so important to us that a promise be fulfilled? Simple: a promise stirs expectation within us of what and how that thing would make us feel.

As an example, a child's parent promises him or her a gift or toy for Christmas, but the promise isn't fulfilled. The child is then left crying because his or her expectation wasn't met. It's the same when we put hope in someone we have trusted for a long time but whose word no longer can be trusted.

Getting past broken promises and purposes can take a lot out of us, if we are willing to change the outcome of the situation rather than allowing it to take us down. The time frame for moving past broken promises and purposes is not the same for everyone. This may well be the beginning of the test of our patience on how far we intend to go to overcome. The joy of overcoming the situations is found at the end. This is the time when we are happier than at the start.

> The heart that constantly hears the words of excellence within may be diligent in pursuing the change and mind-set of self-pity.

Too many times we have toiled in trying our ambitions, pushing our faith forward to overcome the setbacks that have plagued us. Now is the time to take a stand—a stand to demand a change from the bad to the good things that we can attain. A stand when we say no to the voice of the past and yes to the voice of the future for change. A stand that we all can feel within us to break forth out of the things that have weighed us down and changed our personalities from a state of resentful solitude.

Some people long to move on but are paralyzed by fear of doing the things they have the ability to do because their will is locked down. They fear what the outcome might bring them.

A lot of people fail and can't get up because they allow the words and thoughts of other people to paralyze their will and ambition. If we see the problem as being bigger than us, it will always be, but if we change that thinking and start working on the concept that we first believed, it will now give way for change. Never let your problem seem bigger than you are. One chance of giving in to change can go on forever.

God wants to lift us up and out of these broken promises and purposes to give us new ones—ones in which we can have hope, no matter what our past, marriage, life situation, or childhood has been. It is no longer a diminishing force of discouragement. When we come to the point where we can stop feeling sorry for ourselves and do something to change the outcome, we will realize the strength stored up within us. And so it is true that many toil from failure and heartache because they sought favor in unfavorable places, but change is possible and is coming.

Life doesn't always remain the same; things change and adapt. Wake up out of your fears. If you still know your purpose and you still want to fulfill it, keep your will alive to do so. Know this: God loves keeping things secret until the right time to make it seen and felt loudly. Get up now out of broken promises and purposes, and live out purposefully the life that you were called to live.

Hindsight, Insight, Foresight

Hindsight, insight, and foresight—put these three together, and you will see where you have been, where you are, and where you hope to be. Remember how things were when you were a child. Now that you've grown, who would have thought that things would happen the way they have?

It is important that we understand hindsight, insight, and foresight in all things. Hindsight brings alive in us memories and moments of the past that are not all bad. Insight reveals to us who we are and also who God is in us. Foresight gives way for guidance for the future, in which all things should be prepared for a way that has its foundation in the past and present. We shouldn't always look down on the past but at times see it as a way forward that God brought us through. One day we may see the true reason for the things we have been through, so in our present we prepare for all times ahead. Our lives should always be in order so we can master all things that seem to be masters over us.

How did we look at life? Were we only looking at the present and forgot the past, to where we are now will bring alive our past hurts again? How are we looking at life? Do we see what is set before us as it truly is, or have we tried to understand the things we can before it is too late? Consider hindsight, insight, and foresight from where you are at present, to where you will be taken by the grace of God for your life forever.

Vision of the Visionary

As visionaries of Christ our goal is to be successful. If you've never had a vision about accomplishing something for the Kingdom of God, now is the time that made the chance possible. Also if you have been confused about a vision concerning your called purpose now is the time to sort it out before God. We all carry a vision within us, one that we long to see fulfilled. What vision are you carrying? Is it worthwhile? Will it bring you to a better place than where you now stand?

The vision and the dream are within us, and how we attend to them will determine the outcome. The vision and dream of our heart's desire may be broad, but we must remember to allow God to be the central part of it. He knows the desires of our hearts, how big our dreams are, and to what extent we are willing to take it, and so He will help us, even as we commit the thought of it from the beginning (Psalm 37:5; Proverbs 16:3). Committing the very thought of it to God is key, as He will begin to align things to accommodate us. He will work things out according to His will and not in a way that could cause us to falter or lose faith in Him. However, our faithfulness is demanded.

God sees what we can't see and has already seen the outcome. Our determination will take us to all the stages of growth—growth in that He will open doors and make accessible the opportunity. When we put our hands to it, we truly can achieve it if we believe—and keep on believing from stage to stage (Psalm 1:3).

Foundation in all things is paramount, as this is what we build our dreams and visions upon as one thought or imaginative idea leads to another. God corresponds His ideas and imagination to ours when we submit ourselves to Him by listening. Nothing stands alone; there must be something to bolster it from the very beginning. From the beginning we gain strength by trusting in our hearts that with Him all things are possible. As we live in a world today of giant thoughts and ideas, many can't seem to reach because they have no foundation set and can't get there because they have given up on their dream and vision. Every step forward is a way ahead, but many of us falter by quitting something that has a greater outcome. If we let God be our foundation, then He will also be our inspiration.

Around the world today, we can see big things that God is doing. If our dreams and visions are in motion, then we can move things from being just a thought plan to a working plan.

When the mind and heart are open to receive, so shall they be filled with words and thoughts that could become actions.

Mirroring the image of things that come to mind by taking note of them can be a step ahead to give us brighter new ideas. From the picture, ideas, and imagining of things to the hands of the professionals and how we desire things to be, our plans are done in preparation for the future and not just the now.

Vision is not only for the now but for the future, as every visionary's objective is to obtain the maximum authenticity, efficiency and effectiveness, ensuring that incompetence and imperfection is not part of the plan. Our faithfulness in things can cause God to help us become well doers in many tasks within our calling. (Consider, for example, the talent scenario in Matthew 25:14–29.)

That's what God wants to do—to bring out the fullness of Him in us and not give us less than what we are capable of accomplishing. Working along with Him keeps us ahead of things, as He preserves our way ahead. Of course, there will be times when things seem to go wrong, but He will work things out and give us even bigger and better visions of things. Visionaries see things as if they already are accomplished and nothing stands in the way.

When we are young in God, it is always good to allow Him to give us the dreams and visions and see them come to fruition, just as with Joseph. Sometimes when He gives us the vision no one else sees or understands, until it's time of fruition (Psalm 25:14). Starting off at a young age, it's not always easy when things we were not expecting come our way, and we must deal with it to move ahead to a better, more secure place.

As new young strangers in God, learning things early will make us wiser in things of the spiritual and natural/physical so we are better able to balance both and not lose focus later in life. Staying focused in all things is of key importance as we follow up with prayers before Him. Now we can ask ourselves the question, "Am I failing because I lack knowledge, or is it all because I have no foresight/or vision?" (Proverbs 29:18). Birth that vision and dream, and be desperate and determined to fulfill it.

"And whatsoever ye do in word or deed, do all in the name of the Lord Jesus, giving thanks to God and the Father by Him." Colossians 3:17

Joseph's Dream to the Mission

Joseph, the first son of Jacob with Rachel, was given a dream by God, in which the future held the fulfillment of God's plan of redemption for the children of Israel, as well as security and provision. Joseph received this dream when he was about seventeen years old, and it came into fruition when he was about thirty.

Although he had eleven brothers, God chose to give Joseph the vision to fulfill the mission ahead. God showed no one else, although Joseph proclaimed it to his father and brothers. His words, however, were not accredited, and later he was called "the dreamer." Then God gave Joseph another dream to affirm the first so that he didn't lose confidence and begin to doubt.

God showed him the dream before he entered into the mission. He went through a process where he lost everything to gain everything to lose nothing. His test was long and daring, but God was with him. He went from being almost killed to being placed in a hole by his brothers because of jealousy to being sold for twenty pieces of silver. He went from being falsely accused of rape by Potiphar's wife to losing his position as overseer in his house and then being placed in prison until the word of God came for his release—and that changed his life forever. God raised him up to be governor over Egypt to preserve the life of his father and brothers, and he acquired more than he could have fathomed. No more was he bound with chains. No more did he wear prison clothes, and he wasn't locked in a dungeon. His faithfulness and loyalty was reciprocated as God placed him in the position he was destined to fill.

At first, Joseph did not understand the dream that led to the mission and the fulfillment of the dream, not until his brothers came to Egypt to buy grain, and he revealed himself to them. All through the process, God was building Joseph up, as He was with him as the dream was still alive in him. Even though it took a while for the dream to come to pass, it finally did at the time when God wanted it to be fulfilled.

Our lives may be similar as we wait upon God, which may seem to last a long time, but faithfulness in the process will bring God's reward. Maybe He is taking you on a journey, like Joseph (a Josephic Journey), to acquire knowledge and gain insights so you can be used on another level. Hold on; don't give up.

Even though things may take time to be fulfilled in our lives, our faithfulness and trust in God will get us there, and He will be with us, as He was with Joseph. Keep your dream alive, and don't throw it away when it is but a hand's grasp away (Philippians 1:6).

Clean and Clear Conscience

We wrestle at times over the choices in our minds. Sometimes we win, and sometimes we lose, but we should never quit. We must understand where we faltered so that next time, the victory will be ours. We must keep a clean and clear conscience, one that has life in it, one that has peace in it, and one that does not make us feel guilty over the choices and decisions we make.

There exist beautiful choices that give us a clean and clear conscience. A clean and clear conscience doesn't offend; it has standards in place for how we should conduct ourselves. It is all about training the mind to have the power to say no or yes. A daily meditation on the Word of God will give us a way forward for a clean and clear conscience. We have the power to change things or to allow things to change us, but we can establish this power by understanding and building our foundation of a sound mind in Christ.

Our thoughts may bombard us and change our feelings so that we can't keep up with the many things we have to deal with in our lives. It is easy to get things done properly when we have a clean and clear conscience that does not see itself as defeated by anything it is up against. Keep a clean and clear conscience.

My Place in God

Is your name registered in Christ? If so, now is your time to find your operative place in God. It is good to be called a Christian but better when we know our place in Him leads to our functionality in all aspects of our lives.

Every man and woman in God has a place to fill, and in that place are things of the kingdom of God and of our own individual lives as well. Our place in God brings out our position that within ourselves, we can be assured that we have a function.

What qualities do you possess? Are you making good use of them? How do you deal with your words when you have found your place in God? Do you say but not do, or do you say and hope somehow that God will just push you forward without being submissive to Him?

We are saved for a purpose, but first we must know God's place in us—is He in first place in your life?—and know our place in Him. God has endless ideas and missions, and for each of our lives, He has prepared a calling, whether great or small. He is the rewarder.

> *The seeker who sought his or her place in God, having found it, is the heart of foundation that the throne of God's purposes will be well established.*

The strength of our place in God lies upon our faithfulness to Him. Are we faithful in what He says to do? Are we faithful in our own individual lives, so that when He looks at us, He sees a reflection of who He is, with continuance on our part? Knowing our place in God is something that Christ has given as a gift to every person called. We are not just Christians without a purpose or a mission. Weighing our potential and skill together with our will before God in prayer shows that we understand where Christ has placed us as a friend of God. Ask Him where your place in Him is, and He will show you. (Jeremiah 33:3)

We must be true to our own words so that they will prove whether we are weak or strong when it comes to keeping them before God. When we have found our place in God to function, He will then push us to a new vision or dream. Let us not sit back waiting for God to make known what our place in Him is. First, we must be compliant to Him.

To know our place in God is to know ourselves. Know yourself and search out your own life before Him in spirit and in truth—that is, all your weaknesses and strengths. Finding your place in God will help you find your place in this life. Where more can be done, more should be done, and when one is given much, much is expected of him or her until the person fulfills that thing to the very end.

God starts things in our lives—after we know our place in Him—until we have fulfilled what He has called us to do. Every will, purpose, and potential can be added, and He can continue and further the things He has started. Christ was and still is our best teacher by example that we ourselves can follow. Looking at Christ's life on earth, we can be assured of learning some valuable lessons that are fitting for our lives also. Christ knew His place in God, being His only begotten Son, and He went all the way to fulfill what He was sent to do. Of course, He was weary physically and tested, as we now are, but He kept the faith and stayed focused. He understood His place; therefore, He was able to stay focused. Even as we are likewise tested, we must stay focused in all that we do. Wherever we go and whatever we do is a testimony of our lives.

No one should settle for failure, depend upon God, calling upon Him at all times, asking Him to prepare and preserve your pathway of life. We must also ask Him to go before us with His Spirit to do so. It is important to know where we stand, how we stand, and when we stand in our place in

God. It is key to acknowledge the truth for what it is. The knowledge of God is not by what we have learnt and have been taught only but the operation of the Spirit in our own individual lives. The Word of God is proven and is without weakness, so applying it to our lives should be a process of progress of which we can surely testify.

With every purpose, there is a mission, and it is not about depending on one person but every person working together, having the same mind-set as the Spirit gives the ability. Sometimes we have to wait for the Spirit to move us in our place in God, after having built a steady foundation to start with. The things to which God calls us have power and strength that may have started as weakness. Now, the power and strength have grown by continually applying them.

At times, the things for our lives in God are kept secret, not revealed until we build up certain levels. The things that are hidden in Christ depend on our willingness to comply. Our lives are hidden in Christ and still will be revealed in Him. God doesn't want to expose too much before our time without proper foundation, lest after a while pride becomes a driving force in our lives, shaking the steadiness of our foundation. The Word said that "He will never leave nor forsake us", so the compliance of His Word depends on us, as well we acting upon it with obedience and trust.

As we seek to find our place in God, we must always remember that He is our overseer, working things according to His will and purpose. It is He who orchestrates things, along with our willingness and time spent in prayer before Him. He sees the beginning of things as well as the end, and so He prepares us for that which is to come.

Our earthly mission is heavenly geared, not just to please ourselves but to let God be pleased with what and how we do things. No mission of God in our lives is for all of what we want things to be or to benefit our lives only. The mission must never be separated from our place in God because at the end, it's all about Him and us with regard to all things. No more should we wonder where our place in Him is and where His place in us is. We should know and understand that by His Word and going before Him is where all things start and are completed (Ephesians 2:19–22).

Wait on God

The things that are expected to build us up to where God has placed us would take patience from within. Although we may have everything worked out in our minds and hearts, we must go through the process of waiting on Him. This is the place where we build up ourselves spiritually and don't just sit idly, hoping and then saying, "God, use me." Waiting on God, even when everything seems to be in place, is key for us to reach another level and continue steadfastly.

While waiting, we pray, as the Holy Spirit will have us too. We cannot think that we have everything worked out and that waiting on God seems to take too long. We should consider this: whose foundation are we building? Is it ours, or is it God's. He will better use those who are waiting on Him. Though we run the race on earth, He prepares the tracks, and so He looks ahead to ensure that we reach the very end as winners. How did the great men of the Bible reach the place where He had them to be? This was simply by waiting and submitting themselves to Him. This is a lesson for us all. Wait on God, and in waiting, submit yourself so that what you put out is what will be attained—and even more. And as we learn to wait, we will become stronger in prayer.

"Wait on the Lord; be of good courage, and He shall strengthen thine heart: wait, I say, on the Lord" (Psalm 27:14).

Section 3

Looking at Life

Looking at life turns our attention to focusing on the true meaning of a life, from the one we formerly lived in sin to the one we now live toward a hope in Christ, upon which faith is built.

"To See Life—Looking at Life"

As much as knowledge and understanding comes to each of us, we will see life by the approach we take to look at it, How we use the knowledge and understanding we attain will prove if we are progressing in wisdom. "To See Life—Looking at Life" tells the tale of our lives—from how we were brought up seeing life to how we view it now that we have grown. If we listen and observe, we can see how people from many backgrounds see life just by looking at it. The question is this: is there a right or wrong way to look at life, or should we just be thankful for living life each day as a moment to be remembered, without considering God's facts, affirmed in His Word, toward the direction we are heading?

"The Ways of Life"

Apart from seeing and looking at life, we go deeper by understanding the ways of life as it rotates and turns around us, and we grow from each stage and phase. Life has many callings, and not all the ways are the same, though in a good mind-set we aim to be successful in achieving all our goals. It is better to adhere to the ways in which God destined the ways of life to be, apart from the way we suggest it in the standards we live by. We will see that within each of our hearts, there are ways we can't all follow. The ways of life at times may not seem to be to our advantage or bring us to a better place, but by reconsidering and reevaluation, ample time gives us clearer insight.

"The Life, the Process"

Life is a process, and the wise can affirm that. A person's heart is like a castle that he or she builds. By understanding, as time passes, the heart explores things of value where it is much more secured. No castle is built in a day, and so in this life, every process leads to progress that strengthens that foundation. God is our processor, and we are the vessels prepared for whatever mission to which we are called.

"Life in the Flesh, Life in the Spirit"

This speaks to the very soul of our beings as we have one choice and two minds unto eternity. I speak of salvation, which is at the forefront of our lives, whether we prefer to live life in the flesh (of sin) or to live life in the Spirit. Each life lived has power behind it to keep us strong, according to the one to whom we answer the call, but only the life in the Spirit secures the soul's salvation. This draws the line of separation on whether we have found life without God or with Him. God being in or out of the picture brings two different outcomes.

Why Life, Why Death?

The moment we become aware of ourselves, the meaning and purposes of life are revealed. We understand that we are dependent beings when it comes to death, the moment when we reason and weigh the worth of our souls. If we look to life by building up our hope for this life only, when hope is taken from us, what state are we left in? We do not like to lose something precious to us. Just the same, whether we lose our souls or keep them in Christ for eternity, the value comes to light. Though there are many philosophical and ideological concepts about it, some in contention to God's written Word, at the end, His Word still stands.

To See Life—Looking at Life

Many want to see life and look at it from the different callings it proposes to them. This chapter opens to us the concept of seeing and looking at life from a godly perspective that fulfills all things—not for the now only but the eternal just the same as God looks at it from an eternal perspective. As we look at life, we find there is a contrasting wisdom: (1) the wisdom of God; and (2) the wisdom of the world, which is foolishness to God, leading many to hell.

The diversities of life have many of us curious to see life, to experience it, and many have seen it and tell a story. On the other hand, many look at it by the wisdom of the world (which has nothing to do with God). This is the wisdom that has its standards held by the "to do and say as we like", with the absence of reverence of God's commandments as its guide and as a life preserver.

As we grow older, we may be concerned with our dreams and goals. We are in a state of progress by time to get there where at least we can attain a peace of mind with the outcome of things working toward our favor. We are to wait on God—by this I mean praying—so He may show us the clear pathway to that which our lives should be, even if it means learning to deal with frustration and not being distracted or tempted into submission.

To see life at large is to look at it through the ways of God that have a meaning that encompass the satisfaction of the present and the future. We are not here only to satisfy or fulfill the "now" of our lives but also to give way to the fulfillment of the future/ eternal.

Understanding our now will help us to understand and prepare for our future, as long as God's will and mission is revealed to us.

When the eyes of our hearts see life, we are moved to respond to its various callings, but keeping the moral standards can be considered as ethically sound discretion.

As time draws closer to the mission, the vision of achievement becomes clearer. God longs to show us what He has desired us to be and what He has called us to fulfill. He calls as many as will answer, and as long as we submit to the vision revealed, we then can be set on our mission. Time is in the hands of God, which all things concerning Him for our lives should be. This, however, does not mean that waiting becomes us sitting back, hoping that something extraordinary will just happen, while we do nothing. God is a God of foundation. As the Bible says, "If the foundation be destroyed, what can the righteous do?" (Psalm 11:3). We are to build a foundation in Him that can be maintained through anything that comes up against what He desires.

Life is not without choices; we are faced with them each day. Our view of life tells a lot. It tells whether we truly love God; it tells of the hurts and pains others have to bear. It also helps us to understand our destiny eternal—where our souls will rest if we remain ignorant of His guiding light. Starting at a young age in God is preparedness for the future, as He holds the outcome of our choices and decisions in His hand. Early developing a relationship with Him can only bring out our best. Looking at life, now that we have seen it, can help us to remain in the truth that has been on our side through the words Christ spoke.

Are we looking for life to change for the better or are we *waiters of change*, so that all our goals and dreams are held up before us but not in the safety of God? Sometimes we wait for change to come before we start doing things; we're not convinced that the change starts within us. We may be optimistic, but we must allow our optimism to move from a standstill to one in motion. If we are prophetically inclined and watchers of the times, we may see that something is about to change—the awaiting and witnessing of Scripture.

How far should we go to see life? Are we going far enough and reaching forward to the utmost in God, or are we going only as far as to the fulfillment of things for our lives? How and when do we begin to see life the way God sees it? We do so by aligning our lives in the comprehension of His Word.

We may try to see life to find life. Observing what life is in God and what is of the world is important to us all. The ways of God are filled with wisdom from above that cautions us from the ways of the world in the broadness of its callings here on earth. Life is provocative, but a life in God has a greater reward, as He has given the measurement of eternal bliss. We may know and understand that, and sometimes we listen, but we stand in ignorance of the things He offers. Life has its measure, and God knows the end of it. Viewing life without looking at it through the eyes of God is looking in vain and has no eternal profit. As much as we may exercise our power to make choices and decisions, one day there will be no more choices. God will have the final call.

As much as many of us may have our own interpretation of what life is or what it seems to be, the truth is that God's Word has the final say, and every person must face up to that. Every moment is in time and every time is of a moment, whether we remember it or forget it. We can't stop time, and in it are the choices that lapse and hang on every decision that will alter our lives in some way. From youth to elder age, we will all have a story to tell of how we have seen life, now that our lives are lived. Above all we have seen and been through, we cannot ignore the fact that God has already seen the end. No other way than looking at life through His way—from the One who is the future Himself, Christ Jesus—will secure us and guarantee us eternal hope.

God's understanding is above ours, and by it He gives us ways to prepare for the things He has waiting for us. We can't escape life because it is right before us. Whether we live or die, there is a way in which God's power goes past the control of all things so that we aren't forgotten before Him.

Though our lives are set differently and our objectives call us to fill various spaces in life, there is a set way (the God way) for us to live, even if we go off course. Whether we die in sin or in righteousness, God is still the one we will have to face some day. So what shall we say to life, now that we have seen it and looked at it?

Some See Life

Some see life as attaining it all (living for the moment), sometimes without considering the consequences of future outcomes. Some see life as an advantage, where they are in the position to make critical decisions that determine how things should go to their will. Some see life as a mystery waiting to be revealed, of the things hidden in the days ahead, of the things planned and hoped for. Some see life as another opportunity to get an advantage, to see good things come to pass that all of humanity can respond to.

Some see life as a disadvantage and misfortune in the things they have done poorly in the past, which at present seem to have taken a toll and also of things they wish they could get away from. Some see life day by day, hoping to get farther from the point where they are to a higher position where time can be more at their disposal. Some see life as doing things now, with understanding that from here on, they may build upon it for the good of others.

Some see life with abundance, while others see it as sufficient. Let's say you've gained it all, and you stand at the pinnacle of success. Decision and choices are yours. Anything and everything your heart desires is at your fingertips. You call all the shots, you're on top, and you've made it. Nothing stands in your way or deters you. Life is great now. The question left to answer is this: are you satisfied with the state of your soul, the inner you? Chances are you may be satisfied with the state of the body, but deep within, the soul may be hurting.

Some see life from a reality perspective, while others from both a reality and spirituality perspective. Some see life depending on God, while others live from day to day without the thought of God. These days many are living as legends of legacy; that at death, they will be remembered for the things they did and accomplished, for setting milestones for which they are praised. If they lived and died in Christ, surely their souls would rest in peace. We have to weigh our souls in the balance of true worth and merit, whether to the praise of men or having it written among those who have it written in heaven. This brings our souls' worth in deep questioning and debriefing before God.

Apart from the way we all see life and live accordingly, God also sees life as a way in Him, that by wisdom, if we obey Him through the truth, we will come to see it as He does—from an eternal perspective.

The Ways of Life

Up and down are the challenges we face in this life, those that we expect and those that we don't expect. As the many ways of life change every day, faith is most needed. Faith allows us to keep good ways prioritized amidst bad circumstances that resound forever in God.

The ways of life are before us, regardless of situations, circumstances, and our different places of position in life. With change taking place around us, we are apt to be careful and watchful in the way things affect us. We can't always run away from choices and decisions; we are faced with them each passing day. Some of us are just starting off in life, and some are trying to catch up with life after past failures and wasted years. Some are just going through the motions of life, with little or no ambition, and some depend on the aid of others because they can't help themselves.

> One way or another comes the thoughts and actions of our choices, leading to and opening doors to the future ways in the life we chose.

The ways of this life are as a growing divisional line of choices and preferences that differ between the youths and the elders of this generation that the things that are more appealing are for a younger generation to be fond of interest and/or is becoming exceedingly common. As much as things are the way they are, each of us has a calling to a spiritual and physical way of life, and not being ignorant that even in the spiritual there is a division of good and evil, and each is great. The kingdom of God, however, is for the saving of lost souls from hell and the kingdom of the devil. Upon this earth we are affected and influenced by both doubt and belief. God has made the truth clear of what Christ accomplished by His death, though many disbelieve and debate the fact that there is even a God.

In this life, we seek a form of happiness and comfort, hoping for a chance and choice in the things we put forward to achieve. It's true that some days seem better than others, and by the slightest change of our thoughts, our feelings can change. Sometimes the way of life might be so dreaded (and it's understood by God) that our hearts comfort can become frozen (as if threatened), and we seek even more, as we are in search of a way out to find peace in our hearts.

As we grow older, our needs, wants, and desires are altered because of how our lives will be functioned or will be operated by it. Some people's lives appear easier than others, as some have to deal with bad things from the past that spill over on others. We must be careful of the things we allow in our lives, lest they create a way for us to live that later is filled with regret and contempt. I call this *age with ways*.

Individually, the ways of life may seem to be a concealed and closed book, and we can't see ahead. The things we sometimes prepare for ought to be changed just to accommodate us. It is as if life has its own hidden agenda, and some things that come our way are not always appreciated or profitable for us. From life's lessons, we learn (either by error or mistakes made) that with a modified approach and application, we can prevent ourselves from falling over in a similar predicament again.

The ways of life can be so delusive that we can become insensitive to the fact that God is looking at our lives and that there is an awaiting judgment that will come as our life files openly reveal both good and evil.

This is the life of real people facing real-life situations, needing real solutions; an eternal hope can only be found in Christ. Everything we do has a determining effect on our lives, either for the greater good or for the worse. We cannot ignore the things in this life or hope they will just go away; we have to analyze each situation and problem and then deal with them.

The ways of life are changing (as much as the things and needs of our lives differ) because of technological advancements and media amenities. To deal with these things we need an ongoing understanding. Things have advanced in this century that people without ongoing knowledge are left in the dark of misunderstanding. This is the way of life that is so vast before us; each contributing factor is an element that will affect our lives and provoke our thoughts in both choice taking and decision making. Believe it or not, it's true and is before us all.

Are we hoping for greater things from this life if our eyes are turned from Christ or are we hoping that life will favor us and open itself to us, and everything we want will go our way? We must put a tab on our hope—where does it stand and in whom does it stand? Will it stand the test of time throughout all eternity? Even the best man standing in God is dependent upon Him, and so we need each other's shoulders as faith keepers to tackle life's situations.

So Says the World, So Says the Word of God

The world has a voice that is tremendously appealing and so does the Word of God. By discovery, we can relate if somehow we have been influenced. They both offer options of many things that our lives can turn out to be—from the Word, good; from the world of sin, bad.

When the Word says to us that "life is found in me; just give a chance now to believe," how can we doubt? So says the world in its treachery to "live life by the painted standards imagined in our minds, knowing that we are in charge of the choices we make."

So says the world, "there isn't a God." To whom, then, do we bring the value of our souls to inspire, guide, and direct? Do we then look to ourselves? Do we trust our instincts on the basis of eternal life? Do we allow the world to define us, the indiscretion of which becomes a trend in our lives so that we can't think ahead?

Though we serve the world in some way or the other, we are not servants to it in sin. The world says many things to us to which we must pay close attention. So also does God, of which there is the guarantee of life eternal. The world has a call, and so does the Word of God. The world calls us to fulfill the now, but God's Word calls us to fulfill both the now and the future in Him.

The Life, the Process

Life is a process from every stage, to every phase, to every step, and when we are given this life, living in Christ, we go through a process to be more of who He is in us and less of the flesh of who we are. This chapter will enlighten us that foundation is the bedrock and security that keeps us moving ahead from an immature to a mature start.

Now that we know our place in God, it's much easier to stand and defend (Galatians 5:1). God is bigger than life and all the challenges it entails. Step by step and day by day, we ought to let Him guide us through it. Sometimes the challenges themselves seem overwhelming, as if we will drown in them. We may even begin to ask ourselves, "Is this what life is?" We all have to face up to life's challenges, whatever they are and however big they are. At times it may seem as if we have no strength left to continue in the thing we started. It's as if all our inner strength and potential is at a standstill.

The life and the process of whatever we want to achieve is not always easy. It may seem as if things are working out one way and not the other. These are the lessons that will prepare us for what may be ahead. There is no shortcut in the process, and if there seems to be, it may be a shortfall later. No one reaches higher from the ground up without a steady foundation, which proves that time, with patience, can now affirm "the life, the process" in God.

Being a Christian faced with these challenges, it's good enough when we call upon God for help (Psalm 121:1–3). Our help is in Him, and if we trust Him, He will always come through for us, even on time. Everything takes time, and being in haste without being properly prepared could slow things down. In observing the life of Christ, we see that He went through a process until the time came when He went out fully.

Even the disciples were groomed by Him that they might have a foundation for what was ahead.

We will always have to deal with something in the future and make some adjustments, but as we remember that God is our builder and Christ is the Author and Finisher of our faith, He will always look out for us to ensure that all things are fulfilled, according to His heavenly will (Psalm 127:1). When we

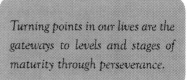
Turning points in our lives are the gateways to levels and stages of maturity through perseverance.

understand that God is in the process, we surely will have a perfected end. He can use anyone when that person commits to Him. Commitment means endurance through all things, while at the same time being faithful and moving ahead in the things that He will now commit to us. Going forward and not looking back or hindering ourselves with things that can cause an ultimate fall is truly exercising wisdom in God. Considering what the eternal in Him will be like encourages us to endure and continue where we have started.

Sometimes when we know what we want to achieve, it's as if we're seeing the clear vision in our minds. There will be things that we must cross over and go through by faith to get there. Our utmost is not limited to ourselves only, as we think of how far we will reach, but truly it is in God to determine how far He will take us. At salvation in Christ we must pursue and keep all things He offers us so we can grow, learning daily how to deal with different and changing levels of situations as life goes on being alert with continuous faith in the wisdom of God. This faith will help us to stand strong, even in faithless places, to handle compromising situations that we can't seem to cope with on our own. When we have gone through this process, that's when we're much stronger and wiser and have attained the knowledge to carry on to where God leads us next.

When we are close to God in spirit and in truth, He will always prepare and move us on to the things that are ahead in a changing society, while keeping us strengthened in it. Time isn't changing unnoticed by God so that His word is no longer as useful as it was several years ago or that we are unprepared to have efficiency and effectiveness in what we are about.

Walking as Christ walked is all good when we make Him the center of what we are about in this process. No one should start off with Christ and end up on their own because that person chose his or her own way in things and ignored the leading of the Spirit. It is the Holy Spirit of God that brings us into the fullness of the will of God in all the processes of this life. Understanding this and keeping it in mind by submitting to the Spirit's leading will always keep us in the perfect will of God.

Staying Focused on "Now"

Some of us have tried to stay focused on the straight pathway, but we must always remember that if we ever go off track and can muster the ability to get back there, we must humble ourselves in doing so.

Why do the strong get weak sometimes and the weak get strong? Why does it seem that we have the ability and the know-how to stay focused, but we still falter? Staying focused can be challenging when the environment doesn't remain the same and is not conducive to our adjusting ourselves so as not to be brought down by the challenge.

By weighing the aspects of things, we can find what we prefer and what we dislike. How do some stay focused on the very thing they started, while others often seem to be off course? Was it because of loyalty and consistency or disloyalty or inconsistency—or perhaps both, respectively?

It is not always easy for new young strangers to stay focused when they make little use of the things at their disposal to maintain themselves or grow. Growth shows us that we have not settled where we started but have built upon that. Focus brings full attention to the things we know we will achieve by faith. Because we believe, we will make it. We can then stay focused.

Staying focused teaches us to maintain our cause in all things that we learned while growing up that now have a place in our lives.

Life in the Flesh, Life in the Spirit

"Life in the Flesh, Life in the Spirit" compares the inner callings of the wants and desires of the flesh to that with which we discipline our spirit, guided by God's Word of what is truly needed. It's the understanding of being called out from walking in the ways of our flesh to being called to walk in the way of the Spirit of God. Whatever a person procures, after a while he or she becomes perfect at it, therefore becoming perfected in ways that could either nullify or justify right from wrong.

Life in the flesh (in Christian terms) is living in sin, the ways that encompass all that is unholy and unrighteous and that can in no way be justified, condoned, or approved by God (Romans 8:8). Life in the Spirit, on the other hand, is justified and approved by God of His intended will. There is a difference in call of each and a difference in the eternal destination that comes after. The life in the flesh has a will and intention that is to destroy men's souls, while the will of the life in the Spirit is of preservation of an eternal hope in Christ.

We may be led to accept that the way of life is by what we hear, feel, see, aspire, and desire around us (earthly gratification). This is a preconceived deception shortfall of earthly boundaries. As much as life may seem to be trendy in one way to please the things of the natural, there also are things of a spiritual nature, which are of truth, that Christ alone can fulfill. A life in the flesh away from God's ways is as a phase of destruction. There is first the ignorance and/or disbelief and then disobedience, all of which is found in the life of the flesh. At the end of this is death, hell, and eternal and everlasting punishment after the judgment. Hanging between the life in the flesh and the life in the Spirit is a choice—to choose whom we will serve: either God or the world (Joshua 24:15).

Every person living has to face God one day with regard to the life that he/she has lived, whether in the flesh or in the Spirit. This will be a chance without choice, whether or not to choose to be judged. How do we measure good and bad? Do we measure it by the outcome of things that have brought satisfaction to us, or do we measure it according to God's Word? How do we deal with good and bad? Do we deal with it by our own standards, or by God's Word? How do we understand good and bad? Do we understand it by our individual understanding and interpretation or by the Word of God? Do we call good "evil" and call bad "good," or is it hard to recognize both these days? Have we set our own standards to live by, according to the ways of the flesh?

According to how we live, our standards are set, and that determines what awaits us before God. God knows wrong from right in a changing world, and He allows us to take full hold of the things that will keep us. It's not about what we think or what we allow that makes things right and good; it's about allowing things to be based on the Word, which will bring out the good, which it is in truth.

Every way of life has a turning point. If we allow ourselves in the things of the flesh, then it will have a turning point and a way of influence in our lives. If we allow ourselves in the things of the Spirit, it will have a turning point and a way of influence in our lives. Every good or bad thing has its outcome, even if it may not seem so at the time. Life lessons can teach us a lot when we pay close attention to them. Observing outcomes can help us make wise choices and decisions that can give us a life of a secured end in God.

> *The closer to the Spirit of God we are, the stronger in our spirits we will be. The closer to the flesh we are, the weaker in our spirits we will be for a life lived for Christ.*

Life in the flesh is simply the way to hell, the wages of sin being paid off. The life in the Spirit is simply the way to heaven and everlasting life, accepting the sacrifice of death that Christ took for us.

We often see that by the ways of the flesh, many are on their way to hell. It is a bitter thing to live a full life in the flesh and die to hell, when we could change things simply by calling upon Christ—the way, the truth and the life. Each way can lead to age with ways, depending on our choices. The age with ways of the life in the flesh can have a person bound to it in continual ignorance of the truth. The age with ways of the life in the Spirit can bring a person to a deeper and closer intimate relationship with God that can never be broken.

The expandability of the life in the flesh must at all times be denied, and mortified that we are not awakened and taken captive by it again, but instead being free in Christ. Christ has given us His Word and Spirit to sustain and maintain the life that is worth living in the Spirit.

Life Side

Those who love life should pursue it in every way possible, in the way of the "life side"—heavenly and eternally. Life side not only looks at this life, but it encompasses the life that awaits those ahead, and those ahead could be sure of it living for Christ. The other side of life (in heaven) is mysterious for many, but the truth of it is, even now it's experienced by those who knew Christ here on earth and will be until those who remain are all gathered together as one.

If we doubt Christ, then we doubt God, and if we doubt God concerning this, then we have ourselves to blame for our ignorance. The words that Christ spoke were the Father's, and we who believe act upon those words after accepting them. So abundant is the life side of the heavenly to we who are alive in Christ. Those who, by sin, know that they are on the death side should consider this.

As life is freely given, so also death freely comes. He who spoke the eternal word is Christ, and He proclaims that in Him, life is everlasting. The simplicity to the life side's calling is to come to Christ, and from there on He begins to reveal things that we never knew and to which we couldn't have responded because our eyes of understanding were closed. But now, we will see from here on the mystery that waits to be unfolded in us.

Why Life? Why Death?

15

Life and death lies openly before us; it's something we can't deny and something we may face. This chapter brings to us a compound reason why we should live a life in God that keeps us away from living a life that leads to hell's gateway. It unveils the beginning of things and also the end. The end of life on earth for the saved but the beginning of life in heaven, and the beginning of life in heaven is the end of life on earth, passing into eternity.

Why life? Why death? These eternal questions are poised at the soul of every human being. These are simple questions, but they present the reality of inevitability. Sometimes it seems as if we are caught between reality, spirituality, and ourselves, caught in the things that are and aren't. In our composure, we seem to be losing the fight. Understanding is a gift, and overcoming things in life is a challenge that we shouldn't give up on. So the questions arise in our minds: Why life? Why death?

Unsupported by our feelings and emotions at times, we know deep within that we want life—not just in this life but in the life to come, some of the things heard of but not yet seen. Provoked from within to the goodness of God, we keep pressing on as if we have lost something that was so dear to us, only to regain it without regard of the length of time and depth of patience needed to get it. Though sometimes we try to make things fit for our own individual lives, there are others who can't even say why life; why death? When they cry, who hears them? When they weep, who can dry their tears? And though we try to stand for ourselves, some in this life fall even when they are fighting. This is real life, real situations that need a real solution. Truly, in Christ we can find many of these answers, which brings our souls eternal peace and rest.

Life is complicated at times, and we can't always run away from situations. We must deal with them, or they will take a toll on us. There always will be things that we must judge, deciding which can bring us a hopeful outcome.

Why does it seem that we are searching for life when we have it? Or is it that we search for better things so that our lives can be more stable? Life is contrary to death of the physical and spiritual. Death is alive, but someday it will be put to death, fully being swallowed up in victory, no more to pain and afflict those who are alive in Christ (1 Corinthians 15:54).

As much as we desire life and chase after it in Christ, death seems to be running the same race, trying to overthrow us. Death is our enemy, but many disregard that point, though they understand it. Some have interpreted life in their own private understanding and live their lives according to their interpretation. Death and its allies are the things of the flesh that within us must be mortified and curtailed. Death doesn't come through waiting; it comes through striking.

Life is apart from death, so that the things in which we sometimes allow ourselves to be engaged, physically, are the things that will kill and damn us to hell, spiritually.

> The heart that is ready to face life in God will be ready to face death with peace and eternal assurance.

Life is not limited to needs, but the objective of our cause is to meet those particular needs. We cannot overcome this life on our own, but with the help of God, we can. Some may think that because they have moved from a stage of unsuccessfulness or misfortune to a stage of success that they have overcome this life. They will find that they have toppled above the system of gain due to dedicated hard work and learning. The true perspective of this life is in Christ, whether we move from unsuccessfulness to successfulness, is that by wisdom and understanding, we now know that we can't carry the temporal things before us at death. Life upon earth is measured, but life in Christ is without measure. A life of tranquility, a life of peace, a life of joy, a life of hope, a life without sicknesses and disease are all found in the greater gift—eternal life. The only life that has such qualities could only be found in God.

Life and death are two realities and are filled with ideas, opinions, dos and don'ts, thoughts and feelings, with the aim of obtaining something. People's lives are different; there are the rich, who have their own obligations. There are the poor, who try to make ends meet. There are those who are incapable of doing things on their own and need the assistance of others. Some smile with tears in their hearts that others can't see, hoping somehow to get answers. Some may say life has meaning, while others may say it is without meaning. Some may say life is against them, while others may say life favors them. Others may go so far as to ask, "What is after life? Is there something better?"—even when they have doubted the truth in Christ.

God is the answer to life, and life is fully fulfilled in Him alone. Even when the answers to our outcries may seem to be ignored or not considered, or even when it takes a long time for our needs to be met, He hears us and will come through for us. To God be the glory that in all that we go through, there is one to call upon and have hope of finding.

So why life? Why death? It's not just the physical or spiritual death but also the things that we started and hoped to finish—our goals, our dreams, our ambitions, and our aspirations. Life is not a mistake, though we may label the things we do or allow as mistakes, or they may seem to slow us down in our endeavors. Sometimes we may feel that if only we could reverse our past, then we would make wiser choices, and the outcome of such wouldn't be so profound.

Going through life does not happen in an instant, and the things we want to attain shouldn't be a way that leads to death. The Bible says, "Seek ye first the Kingdom of God and all His righteousness and all these things shall be added unto you." (Matthew 6:33) As life is in existence, let us therefore embrace it with the love that God has placed in it, so that in all things we will live after we die/rapture. If a person die, he or she shall live again—and that's only in Christ, no other way. "He that hath the Son hath life; and he that hath not the Son of God hath not life [eternal]" (1 John 5:12). Let us live life no more wondering why life and why death. If our lives are secured in Christ, He will carry us all the way through.

Spiritual/Reality Perspective

Everything in life is connected somehow, when it comes down to this physical and spiritual moment. How can we separate the spiritual from reality, when for a moment, something exists and then it is silently passed away. If we were to judge by the things we see, feel, and hear, it would give way to believing more of the natural than the fullness of life.

Humans being physical in this world of reality have spirits that are both touched and influenced by the spiritual and reality. We can look at things from a spiritual/reality perspective, which causes us to think and search to gain an insight of understanding. Spiritual/reality perspective allows us to look at life as it is, and if we are ignorant of anything, then we allow ourselves to be unbalanced in its true understanding.

We can see that Christ, through reading the Word, spoke of this natural world and also the spiritual world from where He came. He came into this natural world to bring a light of understanding to us. He encouraged us to look past the natural world to the spiritual, which has much more to offer. How do we balance both the spiritual and the natural perspective of life? We are in the natural and not yet fully entered into the spiritual (immortality), so the things that are before us should cause us to consider and then make a move toward the gaining of the spiritual that is to come. This is our spiritual/reality perspective that encompasses all of life.

Section 4

Destiny Eternal

With our minds and understanding opened about life, let's now look at what comes after life. From the "Image of Truth, Image of Illusion" right down to "Destiny Eternal," let's gain key insights.

"Image of Truth, Image of Illusion"
In comparing truth and illusion, we'll understand the validity of both and see how they are contrary to each other. At the end, we'll see which brings understanding and meaning to the standards by which they are upheld. However, when it comes to eternal truth, we base facts of understanding upon the Word of God, which some say are unproven and irrational theories. To many who are in the Spirit of faith (now as Christians), God has opened our spirits to see things from a spiritual standpoint and not just a natural one, as many try to decipher in their methodology. Those of us who live by the truth are believers, though we weren't present when the past things were spoken. Still, we, by faith, adhere to the words spoken and heard that illustrate the perfect images of truth to us.

"What God Offers—What The World Offers"
A comparison of "What God offers—What the World Offers" shows what we are living for and who we choose to follow. For some, God is never in the picture with them in this life. Because life is designed in a way that we can grow up with various choices, many were brought up in a way that the least of God's existence was rarely spoken of. The truth finders, who have found Him, will view this life as a temporal one that awaits eternity, with

hope everlasting—a gift that God Himself offers, apart from all we can do in this earthly life that doesn't offer an eternal peace of mind.

"All Over the World"

Universally, a message has been sent out and is still being conveyed from above by those appointed to proclaim it. All over the world, at an appointed time of acquittal, people will testify before the eternal throne. Many have heeded such a call, while others heard but never gave heed and, instead, held such words as debatable contentions to live by. The reason for such a universal message is to prove that partiality will not be a determining factor by which we will be judged. This chapter's message is of peace and hope that gives the soul assurance of its dependent standing, in need of a Savior.

"Face of the Judgment"

"Face of the Judgment" denotes what the judgment will be like when we are face-to-face with it. This is the cautioning factor that allows us to consider our choices in this earthly life and how we intend to answer for all our deeds. Every earthly thing we do is resounded in eternity and must face the judgment of its validity and merit. This also is the time when forgotten memories will come alive to us in consciousness (even those of sin and after being saved) of when, how, and why we did what we did.

"Destiny Eternal"

The seal that seizes the thought, deeds, and ways of evil or good will meet destiny—the moment and time when all things enter the eternal era of time. Destiny eternal swallows up everything that was temporary and of reality, shutting that door and opening a new door, where a renewal work at the hands of God brings new things to stand and hold fast. By this time, we will know the state and place of our souls, whether shining as a light before God or weeping endlessly in a place where light refuses to shine.

Image of Truth, Image of Illusion

To those who believe the Word of God, it is revealed to us as truth, but the image of illusion paints a picture of the things seen, heard, and felt that may seem compelling and appealing to our human calling and may turn us off from the truth. Truth and illusion are on opposite sides, but only one has a sound eternal standing—and when we taste of the truth, we can then relate to it because God will reveal it in our hearts. We will see the image of illusion only for a while, until it expires in death. The image of truth is upheld by the Spirit of truth, and the image of illusion by the spirit of error (1 John 4:6).

Everything presents itself as an image by what we see, even in our minds, but such images lack the truth that has the outcome for what it's really worth. Every image has a shape and form and is at times painted in various concepts and thoughts, which brings understanding. Our lives are like varying colors that bring to light our tastes or preferences, whether in truth or illusion, and have our lives called to a daily response. As we understand that this life has a physical aspect and a true spiritual aspect, even in Christlikeness we can begin to determine things and weigh the wisdom and worth of them.

> When assurance in Christ is met with morality, truth will find its place in our lives.

In life there is an image of truth by the measure of our faith when we find Christ, and an image of illusion that comes from the perceptions of things, but to understand these things we look at them from the spiritual perspective, according to how God Himself will look at it because He will guide us in all the truth. As real as things seem, apart from the way of life in God, it may be an image of illusion (in the lives of those not yet saved).

Looking at things from an eternal perspective in the present, we can truly make a judgment. Many times we allow things into our lives by looking at what they can fulfill for us at a given time, without most of the time weighing what the consequences might be. We are influenced by many things, and sometimes we jump right into them without doing a background check or understanding how that thing could influence or affect us. It's like we're caught in the middle between right and wrong, but after understanding our place in God, we can make a right choice of what will be to our benefit.

Our ambitions should aim toward the image of truth (which is all truth itself) to which Christ calls us. The scripture puts it this way:

"In whom the god of this world hath blinded the minds of them which believe not, lest the light of the glorious gospel of Christ, who is the image of God, should shine unto them" (2 Corinthians 4:4).

Though things may appear good (that is, the bad), an effect of it might not be felt immediately but could affect us down life's road and at the worst time. The world in which we live has become filled with a desire for instant gratification, so that if we have no self-control, we may find ourselves involved in things we didn't expect and suffer the consequences later from the things we desired to acquire.

The image of illusion is a broad aspect we face daily and could become very trendy in its false hope. A trend of things, even the simplest, might leave a way that can hinder us from moving ahead in life and accomplishing our dreams. As individuals, we know whether or not we are moving ahead or whether we are going around in circles.

When we allow God to be our foundation, even early, and we keep things faithful, He will always look out on our behalf, orchestrating things that we can't see.

The image of illusion's aim is to blind people from being free in the truth of eternal life. It offers the things in the present but has a bitter end tied to it. If we ask ourselves why we live, and we understand that the purpose of our living on earth is not only for the present but to bring us to an eternal expectation, then we can see things clearly, according to the image of truth.

The standards we may have set in our lives cannot alter the truth that Christ declared was the way, the truth, and the life. Christ has planned our lives in the image of truth, but only when we enter the way will we begin to see the clear vision unfold in truth. Time is racing to an end, and we cannot sit back when the moment of truth is before us. We must learn that the changes of sure things to come may happen quickly and unexpectedly—that's the fulfillment of scripture.

The profit from the things of the world offered by the image of illusion cannot be compared to the things that God has stored for those truly in love with Him and who are walking in truth. He uses those who offer themselves to His service in whatever field He chooses. We can become strong by allowing ourselves to be influenced by things that will strengthen us. Every image has a reflection, and our lives can mirror the effect of it.

Our consciousness of God's existence doesn't mean that we know Him. When Jesus is in our lives, this makes the difference between knowing God and knowing *about* God. To be conscious of Him and doing nothing about it is more damaging to our souls than if we ignore the truth. If we are aware of these things but are ignorant about changing them, it is an illusion. We may never change that way of thinking, as things seem to be going well in our lives. This may be a form of godliness in our minds. The time is now for us to move from a conscious state of believing in God's existence to becoming real with Him. Our consciousness will be activated when we do so.

My friend, Christ is the answer to life. Life is Christ, and Christ is life. He prepares you now in this life for the life to come. Though we may be in the world, we shouldn't be of the world, having a form of godliness. Rather, we should be totally immersed in the truth itself. Be careful not to be blinded by the image of illusion because the physical (of sin) is here but momentarily (2 Corinthians 4:17–18). Only the spiritual things of God will have that eternal standing of hope. A God-built life is the foundation of all purpose to life.

Signs of Deception

How can we know and be sure? Do we watch for signs, or are we too busy living life? If we abide in the Spirit, we will have spiritual understanding about the spiritual as God reveals to us for knowledge that we are not captured and held bound by them. It is true that there are signs all around us, but what is the significance? Are the signs meant as warnings and precautions of things that may have a bad outcome? Being careful and watchful of the things that influence our lives is not a bad thing, but it could be counted as a way in which we aim to secure eternal life in Christ.

What are the fulfillments of signs that, from a Godly perspective, we watch for the ways and moves they make? Are they to remove our focus on God and lead us astray by fulfilling something else? Signs of deception must never be ignored, while being connected to God in these days when wrong seems right, and right seems wrong. When God has given us life, He expects us to watch for deception—not that we can control all things, but we should control those things we can, so that one good turn is the outcome of another.

As much as God is there to preserve us in the truth revealed, we also have an enemy who wants to turn us away from it by perverting it so we who are not so spiritually inclined may fall victim to him. If we fall for what may be a deception decoy, we should ask God to help us to overcome it as He watches over our souls in this life.

What God Offers—
What the World Offers

This chapter compares the things that God offers to us to what the world offers to us. If we make a list and weigh their worth, then the comparison process begins. This bears the eternal weight of our souls to the call of the Master. Now we are between choices and decisions that would determine to whom we bow down and serve this day, and looking at things from an eternal perspective will help us in how to make the right choice.

The curtain that hid life before us (spiritually) is now pulled down so we see what it offers. God offers something, and the world offers something as well. We cannot completely close our eyes or turn away from God because He was at the beginning, and even at the end shall He be also.

Though each of our lives is different and the ways of them change from time to time, to everyone something is offered, but how we respond to things can tell and determine what attracts our attention even from deep within. God offers life to us all, even though many today don't believe in Him or find it hard to accept that He exists. The life He offers us is in Christ, from His birth, death, and resurrection. In Christ's resurrection is the perfection of everlasting life that He so longs for us to have (2 Peter 3:9). On the other hand, the world offers the contrary, which involves the way of sin. Though we all live in the world, we can by our choices in Christ, choose not to live in it or be manipulated by its sinfulness. From childhood to elder age, there are things that our eyes have seen and ears have heard, and there also are the things that we have been taught. From the process of all these things, we at a point will have to stand alone in our choices and decisions.

On the whole, what does God offer to us that is so grand that with patience He allows us to come to Him before all things come to an end? We have established that He gave eternal life through Christ. So now, as our individual lives are different—occupying different jobs and vocations and having different challenges to overcome—can we truly use the offerings of God to build our lives upon? Yes, we can. The Word of God is the manual for this life, even in a changing age. We start off with the basics in Christ, and whatever way we are in, He makes us know that He may alter things if changes ought to be made or to give us an added calling in Him. This then helps us to understand and see clearly to what He has called us.

God offers us peace with hope in Him that we can't find nowhere else. The peace that reaches deep within our souls starts here on earth but continues forever into eternal life. This peace is not temporal, of the world, but has an eternal permanence. The world may seem to offer a type of peace, but it is not the peace that is fulfilled in God. The peace that the world offers is temporal; it doesn't continue on when we die. So then we judge the peace offerings. It is wise that we honor God's offering that has no end though the peace of the world seems appealing. What the world calls peace is filled with sin because in it are the ways that will lead to eternal death. We are not mistaken that we are to be peacemakers but not in the effort of sin or contrary to God's Word.

Can our faith endure in the things that God offers us amid the world that calls good evil and evil good? Of course it can. What standards of interest in life do we allow ourselves to procure? Is it of righteousness or unrighteousness that we who are passionate of life are fond of doing? The world is filled with dos and don'ts and wants and needs that have no eternal holding but can only fulfill what is of the now.

> *The eternal weight of God's offerings should be on demand in our lives for peace and love to be openly seen and felt among us.*

Living life only for the moment is the mistake many have made—and still are making. To prepare for the future is to be prepared in Christ, who has already seen both the beginning and the end. Though the world offers everything of the now, it doesn't guarantee eternal life. If the things of our now are based and built upon the things of God, then we can be sure that our eternal mission is fulfilled, but unless it lines up with the things of God, its disappointments await.

Clearly, we can see that the things of the world that are proposed to us, so in our choices and decisions, we must be wise in the wisdom of God. Understanding the things that are around us and not being ignorant of them can help us preserve ourselves in God. The things that He offers may not come quickly but may require a process of patience that our lives ought to be adjusted and aligned. To that everything else is added spiritually and physically.

The Way Up, the Way Down

Maybe not right now but sometime ahead, the thought will return to us, as long as we are able to remember what led us to the way up or the way down. Can we avoid all things that life throws at us? Can we go before time actually reaches us and change things before they have an impact on us? Of course not. When we sit silently and consider things, we can then search our lives so that we can begin to work on things in our lives and for our lives, setting perspective to prospective.

Some people seem to be moving forward in life, while others just don't seem to do so. What do we want for our lives? What do we want in our lives? Do we desire things that offer something better than where we are? Looking at things now, can we even begin to motivate ourselves to get there? How can we tell whether we have moved forward or are stagnating?

Surely everyone wants better things for their lives; it's the very reason so many of us make sacrifices without holding back. Life sometimes is too much like a game—some things play fairly while others do not. Hopefully, the things that we desire most and hope for most earnestly are the things we have to give the most to gain. We don't know how long life will go on, but as time passes and life continues, we strive to make it to the way up and that in Christ by God's grace, rather than giving up and allowing ourselves to be brought down.

All Over the World

Perfect timing, open hearts, a humble and contrite spirit is a call being made all over the world. This is a universal shout to the world to fix its hope and trust in the God of all spirits who can save our souls. He gives grace to the responder to this call.

Now that we understand what God is capable of making of us, He will make a universal call to all those who are not born in Him to also answer that call where His mercy extends, so they can become new young strangers, even as David said he is a stranger to God (Psalm 39:12).

God doesn't want us to waste our lives in becoming the devil's trophies or his prize possessions at the end of our lives by ignoring His warnings. The decision to come to know Christ is more critical than ever because of the desperate times, which we may think are favorable to us. Language, race, or color is not a barrier to the call God is making, but He looks at the heart of all. He makes a call that is certain and is worthy of eternal life and peace.

> *A perfect message to an imperfect heart may see the light of life in its true meaning that cautions us to give heed.*

The ways of the world is sometimes like a trend that with each passing day has its own dealings and callings. Are we waiting for greater things to happen and fall into the alignment to the way of our lives? Are we ignorant to the call? Those of us who have seen the light of the truth and have felt the weight of God's love toward us can understand the intent of the universal call He is making. The value of our lives is higher than we can imagine. We live to see another day, but to understand the value of living to its fullest extent can only be interpreted in Christ. The things God offers us are perpetual and eternal, even as we pass through this temporal world. Many are the ways of this life, and as time passes, spiritual wisdom in God should be greatly demanded and sought. The elements of things that we see are not always interpreted in the way things really are, but closer observation brings clearer understanding. With the wisdom of God, we can be sure that even as each year passes, our faith in Him will not wither but will be progressive in constant growth.

Why does time linger, so the cry that God makes is one of patience with a world whose ways are seemingly diminishing from the pathway of the truth? Can we have all the answers to the questions we ask or even seem to understand the full changes of time? Maybe not, but bit by bit, as we adhere to the truth, we can gain deeper insights. The modernization of things in this life increasingly is on the rise, and as this happens, the demands for the best and most effective things have a part to play. Similarly, we should want the best for our souls and the souls of our loved ones. We shouldn't allow anything to stand in the way or supersede the needs for our souls that have much more worth than anything put together on earth.

Are we ready and prepared for something greater in the future of our lives, which we are incapable of understanding at present? If not so, let's align our souls with God's word that eternal peace, safety and security can be ours to attain. Time has a destiny, and as we are a part of this, so also our choices will either bring us to a place of hope or a place of torment. Christ offers all the world the wealth of eternal life. Though many a time we have fallen weak by our own words and deeds, now that we are made aware of our faults, amending them should be something we should allow God to help us with. We will not just look at things from where we are now but where we intend to be.

The future is before us, and time is in the power of God's hand. He knows what is ahead in our lives, and, with caution, He will answer our humble cries from the heart. We live in the present, but the future is hidden from us, while our hopes are kept alive. Therefore, to hope for things in the future without the future holder is to hope in vain. God has seen it all—the past, the present, and the future—and He knows the phases and stages of all things. Salvation with growth to the future is as a sealing security with Him, experiencing His merciful kindness.

Leaning onto our own understanding, procuring the extent of what life offers, can be challenging, as everything entailed has a calling and an outcome. So then to what and whom would we respond? Will we continue in our ways apart from God, or will we now heed His calling? Can we see clearly to the things that pertain to a life worth living in God, now that we understand not just our physical needs but also our inner souls' calling needs? Shall we now walk into the light, or do we walk away?

As much as we have heard, seen, and felt things in this life, there is much more we will come to conclude. We can conclude that now a perfect message is sent, and we are witnesses to it, but how many will respond to it in the way it was given? The message God sends is clear, and as we answer, it becomes even clearer to us. Responding to God's calling is exercising wisdom, and following His Word is the gateway to understanding. We cannot take the things of God lightly, lest they return heavily impressed upon us, even at a time when we don't expect it.

Eye on the World

God knows who belongs to Him. He claims those who claim His Son. He views the world as we may see it and as He sees it. His eye is on the heart of the world, making Himself available to those calling on Him in truth. He sees the good and the bad that are done, yet by mercy and grace we are not consumed.

Everything is seen in an instant, and nothing is hidden. His eye is on the world, from our hearts, to our homes, and from our homes to our schools and jobs. His eye is on the world from our ministries to our churches and all other things. His eye is on the world of those who cry daily and those who die daily, of those who hunger and thirst daily, of those who are taken captives daily, and of those who pray daily. His eye is on the world and on our lives of wants and needs.

His eye is on the world for lost souls who have not yet touched eternity but linger at the call. His eye is on the world among all people and all things that cross the greatest seas, oceans, and land masses from all over the world. Even as God has His eye on the world, so too does the devil, to proceed in every evil intention. We should not be ignorant of this.

"The Lord is in his holy temple, the Lord's throne is in heaven: His eyes behold, His eyelids try, the children of men" (Psalm 11:4).

Face of the Judgment

There are those who lived among us who have gone from this life, and there are those among us who live daily. However, we shall all one day come face-to-face with the judgment—the time of the trying and processing of our thoughts, words, and deeds.

Given to us is life upon this earth, but how long is our time before it comes to an end? With this gifted life we now live comes all the heavenly warnings of how it should be lived to secure an eternal end with God. Now that we have life, it is evident that eternity is ahead. Any person who has Christ has life, the security of which is eternal and everlasting.

Have we reached the pivotal point where we are no longer convinced of eternal life? The face of the judgment shows us clearly what the great white throne judgment will be like, of those who will stand and those who will be cast away. With the vision of John the Revelator, a picture can form in our minds that aims to alter our thoughts and lives to be one in Christ.

> "And I saw a great white throne, and Him that sat on it, from whose face the earth and the heaven fled away; and there was found no place for them. And I saw the dead, small and great, stand before God; and the books were opened, which is the book of life; and the dead were judged out of those things which were written in the books, according to their works. And the sea gave up the dead which were in it; and death and hell delivered up the dead

which were in them: and they were judged every man according to their works. And death and hell were cast into the lake of fire. This is the second death. And whosoever was not found written in the book of life was cast into the lake of fire." (Revelation 20:11–15)

The mystery of the judgment is extensive and deep, but we must thoroughly examine our lives before God.

The Bible states there is a coming judgment for all of humankind for the things we have done, either good or bad. At this time, God will try our hearts, bringing our deeds to the forefront, either to be rewarded or to pass justice. It makes no difference whether we believe this or not; the fact remains that God's Word is forever settled in heaven and will come to fruition (Psalm 119:89). The face of the judgment should in no way be rejected or ignored because every person who has ever lived will be without excuse for the things he or she has done. This is the moment when people will stand before the Lord of Glory. The nonbelievers will now believe, the disobedient will now confess, and the sinners will be reproved. God will be fair in this; partiality is not a word that will be mentioned in the judgment.

> *The existence of what is to come will seem to be the inexistence to the heart that doubts God's spoken word.*

Now that we know these things that are to come, it is time we make our hearts right with God and before Him, confessing all of our sins. Living with knowledge of knowing the truth in ignorance will make things worse, if nothing is done about it. Christ stands at the door of our hearts, knocking, while the angels stand ready to rejoice as our names are written in the Lamb's book of life, but He will not always knock if we ignore (Revelation 20:15). The seeds we sow in our lives will be reaped at the judgment, so then our reaping is determined by ourselves, but our rewarder is God.

As much as we spend time considering life, we should also consider eternity, where our souls will rest. The gift of life that we have been given is one in which we enjoy the pleasures of God, while staying focused and faithful to Him. If we are faithful, we will stand in the judgment as the faithful, but if we aren't, then all things will be evident of itself. The wise in God will consider that as long as we are in this life, God looks on, and there awaits a coming judgment.

The young as well as the old should consider who God is, know what He stands for, and seek Him daily. What shall we say then to all of these things that are now left before us to believe and accept? The choice of our destiny is in our hands when we choose to believe and obey the truth that God will cover and keep us in Him. We cannot again live our lives without a certain fear and hope for the mercy of the Almighty God. Someday, one day, will be our day, and even as many die and face the judgment, the files of our lives are written in the books that shall one day be opened and revealed. Whether we are new to the faith or have been in the faith for years, we are all counted and will all be acquitted because of Christ's love toward us.

Book of Life

One day the books will be opened, and the written things will be revealed, both darkness of deeds and light of deeds, the good and the bad (Revelation 20:12). The many who are living whose lives are not written in the book of life (this we will know by the lives we live and the convictions we feel within our hearts) can have their names written there.

Our lives await a judgment, one that will bring us to silence as we listen to the things that we have done, said, and thought of doing. All people who are registered in the book of life (by our own choosing) will go unto eternal life, and all who are not registered therein (also by our choosing) will go unto eternal death and damnation (Revelation 20:15). Whether we believe it or not, it is written. Can we truly be sure that our names are written therein? Yes, we can. We can know by living for Christ, and if we are not certain, the decision is open before us (Revelation 3:5). If we are not living for Christ, our names after the judgment will be called to face the eternal consequences. This is not hard to understand. Now we should consider and reconsider our life before we pass from this life as to have our name written in the Lambs book of life being sealed for all eternity.

Destiny Eternal

20

If we live life for heaven on earth, we will have it in heaven itself, and if we live life for hell in the broad ways of unrighteousness, we will have hell itself. Live life for heaven on earth, as destiny eternal closes in on the time left here.

Heaven or hell—two places, one choice. One way and one answer—Jesus Christ, in this lifetime. Have you ever considered where you will spend eternity? Every person living should consider this and not turn away or ignore or come up with any other way but knowing for sure that as we all have lived upon this earth, we are heading for destiny eternal. This is where our time destiny chance comes in.

Everyone living life is prepared for something, even those who live aimlessly and in rebellion to God. Life is a prepared thing; destiny is eternal—a heaven or hell call. We cannot escape eternity; it is something we must all face, but what matters most is how we will face it or how it will face us. Nothing escapes eternity. This is the change and shift of new moments that from eternity we look at life, back to the time we lived upon earth.

As we breathe, we have life, but when that breath of life is gone, we are dead physically. According to a person's way of life lived upon earth, there are two destinations where our souls and spirits can be. As scripture affirms, there is the place called hell, where the lost souls that refused and rejected salvation in Christ's soul will be seized forever, with everlasting burnings. Then there is heaven, where God and Christ dwell, where the righteous in God will forever be, never again to experience the former things that affected them, such as pain, sickness, and death. If we leave God out of our lives, so also is the hope of getting into heaven. Some people make it seem that heaven is without God by the confessions they make, that somehow it awaits them without making Christ their Lord. We should consider the importance of our souls and that the price Christ paid was so heavy. It doesn't take much wisdom to understand this, but by believing in our hearts, faith can take its place.

Everyone living considers some form of security for their lives, away from the things that may seem as a threat to their lives. We want that security that assures us that we can live through this life. In the same way we desire that form of security, the security of our souls is offered by Christ Himself. The only person that can secure someone's soul if he or she dies is Christ, because for this reason, He came and died.

As much as we consider our lives as valued, Christ does even more so, and we can only see and feel the realness of this when we come to Him. There is no other way that we can experience the fullness of eternal life but through Him. If someone's soul is lost, nothing can be offered to God as a payment for the security and saving of his or her soul from hell. Do we measure the things of acquisition to gain the whole world and lose our precious souls? Christ's word is clear and to all it is; as many as will believe and receive Him (Matthew 16:26).

The terror of hell is real, as the Word of God, which cannot lie, affirms and will confirm that. Many don't like to hear about this, but it cannot be denied or ignored.

Because of what it is, people may not want to hear about it or believe that such a place exists—this is to ease their consciences of fear. The worst of this matter is to be lost and have regrets and remorse for the things one has done. Didn't the rich man confront Lazarus and Abraham for pity, for a drop of water, in the parable Christ told? If someone ends

As all things enter life, so eternity has its final say of what things will and will not go on forever.

94

up in hell, that person's conscience will be awakened, but the thoughts can never be executed. Christ forewarns us that it is better to enter life (everlasting) with one hand, eye, and foot than to end up in hell being whole.

Christ knows that hell is wide open for the wicked who willfully disbelieved, ignored, and disobeyed such words that could have prevented them being there. It is upon us to search our lives and consider the current state we are in, the things we do, and the way of our lives that such things aren't overwhelming for us. Is it wisdom to have life with full abundance in the present if it hinders us from coming to know Christ? Hell is a reality, and many should make it their ability to know Christ as Lord and Savior to escape such horror and terror.

Eternal destiny is an important aspect of our lives. The decision must be made forthwith, with the assurance that one has been born again by the Spirit and is now saved (John 3:1–7). Searching ourselves is important before God, as is asking ourselves the eternal question: "Where will I spend eternity?" (2 Corinthians 13:5). Am I in the place to receive eternal and everlasting life in Christ?

The eternal time is placed before us and the choice lingers, even as time in life has been given to us. God does not want us to go to hell. He wants us to be with Him, but we can't have it our way and expect that His way will somehow fit in. This is the reason why Christ knocks at the heart with patience, but if the patience runs out, and we are no longer alive, what shall we say then to these things?

Unto All Eternity

When all our thoughts and imaginations are swallowed up in eternity, then we will look at things from eternity to the time we spent on earth, either in the truth or away from the truth. All things are gathered to eternity, both the good and the bad—gathered for the time to prove and weigh all things both on earth and above.

Where is life heading? Is it heading for deeper and better things, or is it heading for a downfall in an unknown future time? Are we afraid of eternity, wondering how we would stand? Are we waiting for it, or do we, with consciousness, wait for things to happen for us and then believe what was preached countless times?

Christ is the Master of eternity; it is His time to bring all things under subjection, both the things that fill the heavens and the things that fill the earth of the natural and the spiritual. Nothing will go unnoticed, from the foundation of the world until now. Time will stand still at the moment the Master of eternity makes His call from the heavens of heavens, as He puts all things in their proper place, so they shall never again go out of order and coherency. He being the Master of eternity, He will cherish those who loved Him and bore hard things to His kingdom. Those who strengthened themselves as His enemy He will put to shame by their own shame, in which they have willfully engaged. We can't miss eternity.

Anything that moves, breathes, and inhabits the earth will now—having fulfilled its purpose—be in harnessed harmony. To all eternity shall all things be by Him, who was, and is, and forever will be.

About the Author

Dylon Pharez Charles was born in the beautiful Caribbean Island of Grenada. He is the second child of his parents' three boys and one girl. At the age of eighteen, despite life's frustrations and all the glitter the world had to offer, he gave his life to Christ, setting himself apart from the sinful things of the world of which he was fond—which wasn't that easy.

He was brought up in church, but it wasn't until he opened his life to God that a true transition took place. He loves the gospel of Jesus Christ. It is now his mission to share God's love with as many people as he can through writing.

Dylon Charles says, "On August 1, 2001, the Holy Spirit visited me in a supernatural way that changed my life forever." Thank you, and may God richly bless you.

Printed in the United States
by Baker & Taylor Publisher Services